W9-CHP-324

SHARON JAYNES

THE POWER OF A WOMAN'S WORDS

WORKBOOK AND STUDY GUIDE

HARVEST HOUSE PUBLISHERS

EUGENE, OREGON

Unless otherwise indicated, all Scripture quotations are taken from the HOLY BIBLE, NEW INTERNATIONAL VERSION®. NIV®. Copyright © 1973, 1978, 1984 by the International Bible Society. Used by permission of Zondervan. All rights reserved.

Verses marked NASB are taken from the New American Standard Bible®, © 1960, 1962, 1963, 1968, 1971, 1972, 1973, 1975, 1977, 1995 by The Lockman Foundation. Used by permission. (www.Lockman.org)

Verses marked NLT are taken from the *Holy Bible,* New Living Translation, copyright © 1996. Used by permission of Tyndale House Publishers, Inc., Wheaton, IL 60189 USA. All rights reserved.

Verses marked AMP are taken from The Amplified Bible, Copyright © 1954, 1958, 1962, 1964, 1965, 1987 by The Lockman Foundation. All rights reserved. Used by permission. (www.Lockman.org)

Verses marked NKJV are taken from the New King James Version. Copyright © 1982 by Thomas Nelson, Inc. Used by permission. All rights reserved.

Verses marked KJV are taken from the King James Version of the Bible.

Emphasis in Scripture references has been added by the author.

Cover by Garborg Design Works, Savage, Minnesota

THE POWER OF A WOMAN'S WORDS WORKBOOK AND STUDY GUIDE
Copyright © 2007 by Sharon Jaynes
Published by Harvest House Publishers
Eugene, Oregon 97402
www.harvesthousepublishers.com

ISBN-13: 978-0-7369-2150-3
ISBN-10: 0-7369-2150-8

All rights reserved. No part of this publication may be reproduced, stored in a retrieval system, or transmitted in any form or by any means—electronic, mechanical, digital, photocopy, recording, or any other—except for brief quotations in printed reviews, without the prior permission of the publisher.

Printed in the United States of America

08 09 10 11 12 13 14 15 / VP-SK / 12 11 10 9 8 7 6 5 4 3 2

Contents

DIGGING DEEPER

I WAS 17 YEARS OLD. About 25 of my jean-clad friends and I sat crossed-legged on the floor of our Christian coffeehouse called *The Ancient of Days*. Bell-bottom hip-huggers, tie-dyed shirts, long straight hair (on boys and girls), platform shoes…we were a sight. We gathered each week for a Bible study led by a twentysomething fellow from the local college. After singing "Pass It On," the leader grew very serious, lowered his voice, and posed the question: "Who came here tonight to have…fun?"

My hand was the first to shoot up in the air! As a matter of fact, mine was the *only* hand to shoot up in the air. I sheepishly looked around the room and mumbled, "Wrong answer?" I felt as though I had a neon sign over my head blinking HEATHEN! HEATHEN!

With a tsk-tsk look on his sullen face, the young man, just a few years my senior, announced, "We are not here to have fun! We are here to study God's Word."

But what that whippersnapper didn't understand was, for me, studying God's Word *was* fun! What could be more exciting than discovering answers to the mysteries of creation, seeing Jesus revealed in the Old Testament, and uncovering truths that can set you free! The Word is a love story, a murder mystery, a history lesson, a letter from God, and the key to wisdom all wrapped into one. Wow! That is fun. The Bible is filled with treasures waiting to be discovered. It was exciting to me when I was 17, and it is still exciting to me today.

I am delighted you have chosen to dig deeper into God's Word to discover more about the power of a woman's words. And if you are studying this material in a group, I pray that you will...have fun!

How to Use This Study

Except for lesson 1, each lesson is to be completed with the corresponding chapter in *The Power of a Woman's Words*. I realize that some days we have more time to study than others. Rather than break the lesson into days or segments, I have left them intact. However, I encourage you to spread out your study time of each lesson over the course of a week or two weeks.

When God provided manna for the Israelites who were in the desert for 40 years, He gave them a daily supply (Exodus 16:14-24). They could not gather enough for a week and then refrain from gathering the manna on the other days. If they tried it, the manna would spoil. They gathered the life-giving bread from heaven every day (except on the Sabbath).

Likewise, Jesus taught His disciples to pray, "Give us this day our *daily* bread" (Matthew 6:11). God's Word is like God's bread for us, and I believe the best diet is a daily supply. So I encourage you to spend time in God's Word every day. I can hardly wait for the feast! Let's get started.

Lesson 1

LITTLE WORDS, BIG INFLUENCE*

Power verse:

"Likewise the tongue is a small part of the body, but it makes great boasts."

JAMES 3:5

A WORD HAS BEEN DESCRIBED AS the smallest unit of meaningful linguistic communication. But that little tiny entity has great potential.

1. Read James 3:2-6 and answer the following questions.

   How is the tongue like the rudder of a ship?

   Who is the ship? (There is not necessarily a right answer.)

   On any given day, there are many travelers on our ship (our families and friends) or people we pass on the waterways of life. How do our words carry people along the same route we

* Lesson 1 corresponds to chapter 1, "Mixed Messages," in *The Power of a Woman's Words*.

are traveling? How do our words maneuver or bump into those that are passing by?

2. Read the following verses and note how words direct the course of a person's life.

Proverbs 12:5-8

Proverbs 12:13-22

Proverbs 22:6

3. If we want to steer our ship in the right direction, which way do we need to turn the rudder? Read 1 Peter 3:10-11 and fill in the blanks.

"For whoever would love life and see good days must keep his _____ from evil and his _____ from deceitful speech. He must _____ from evil and do good; he must seek peace and pursue it."

This verse tells us that we must turn the steering wheel from _____ and steer it toward _____.

4. What comes to mind when you hear the word "pursue"?

Is the idea of "pursuing" a passive activity or an active chasing after?

How do we pursue peace with our words?

5. Our words are also like the bit in a horse's mouth. Read James 3:3-5 once again.

    Look up and define "bit."

    Describe in your own words the purpose of a bit in a horse's mouth.

    How are your words like a bit in a horse's mouth?

6. When a horse is on his way home from being out in the fields and sees the barn in the distance, he may have a tendency to bolt. The horse is comfortable in his stall and wants to go back to what he knows. It takes a practiced rider to keep such a horse under control and walking at a steady pace.

    How does this relate to the words we speak?

    Who is holding the reins of your bridle?

7. Read the following and note the difference between a woman who is holding the reins and the woman who has handed the reins over to the Holy Spirit.

    Romans 8:5-6

    Galatians 5:16-23

8. One day my husband, Steve, and I went on a trail ride on vacation. After assessing our experience with horses, they assigned each member of the group a horse that fit his or her ability. Steve was assigned Old Slow Joe. As we plodded down the dusty trail, Steve and Old Joe fell behind. Steve coaxed, prodded, and kicked the ancient steed in the ribs, but to no avail. Old Joe was more interested in munching on the shrubs along the road than keeping up with the gang. Old Joe was set in his ways, and no amount of urging from Steve was going to change him.

    Lest you think your horse and pony show is too far gone to change, let me take you to one of the most comical scenes in the Bible. The prophet Balaam was just about to disobey God when He sent a messenger to confront him.

    Read Numbers 22:24-31. Through whom did God speak?

    Was Balaam surprised that the donkey was speaking?

If God can speak through a donkey, then, sister, He can take control of our tongues and speak through you and me as well! (I told you we were going to have fun.)

9. Read and record Proverbs 25:11.

The NIV translation states, "A word aptly spoken is like apples of gold in settings of silver."

Look up the word "aptly" in a dictionary. What new insight do you gather from the definition?

How important is wisdom in determining if a word would be "aptly" spoken?

10. In contrast to "apples of gold," the writer of Proverbs paints another picture of words spoken without discretion. Read Proverbs 11:22 and note the difference.

Both verses compare words to precious gold. However, one is a treasure and one is a waste. Which do you want your words to be?

11. If you are doing this study in a group, consider sharing a story from your own life in which the words of a woman changed the course of your life for a day or for a lifetime. If you are doing this study on your own, use the following space to journal your thoughts.

I can't wait to delve into the Bible to see what God has to say about the words we speak. Let's pray before we begin this journey together.

Dear Father, I know there is great power in the words I speak. I have seen looks of hurt and disappointment when I've spoken a careless word, and I have seen looks of hope and excitement when I have spoken an encouraging word. As I study what Your Word has to say about my words, I pray You will open my eyes to Your power, my heart to Your conviction, my mind to Your truth, and my ways to Your will. In Jesus' name, amen.

Lesson 2

*G*OD'S *I*NCREDIBLE *G*IFT

Power verse:

*"The tongue has the power of life and death,
and those who love it will eat its fruit."*

PROVERBS 18:21

ONE OF GOD'S MOST INCREDIBLE GIFTS to mankind is the gift of words. He could have chosen to give words to zebras, monkeys, or giraffes. But amazingly He chose to give them to mere mortals... created in His very image.

1. Read the following verses, fill in the blanks, and answer the corresponding questions.

    How does Paul describe God in Romans 4:17?

    "The God who gives life to the dead and _____."

    What does that description of God mean to you?

2. How does the writer of Hebrews define "faith" in Hebrews 11:1?

   Do you see any relationship between Romans 4:17 and Hebrews 11:1? When we speak with faith, what are we essentially doing?

3. Read the following verses and fill in the blanks. These verses were taken from the NIV translation. If you are using another translation of the Bible, the words will be similar.

   Genesis 1:3: "And _____, 'Let there be light,' and there was light."

   Hebrews 11:3: "By faith we understand that the universe was formed _____ so that what is seen was not made out of what was visible."

   Psalm 33:6: "By the _____ were the heavens made, their starry host by the breath of his mouth."

   Psalm 78:23: "Yet he _____ to the skies above and opened the doors of the heavens."

   Psalm 147:15-18: "He sends his command to the earth; _____ _____ runs swiftly. He spreads the snow like wool and scatters the frost like ashes. He hurls down his hail like pebbles. Who can withstand his icy blast? He _____ and melts them; he stirs up his breezes, and the waters flow."

4. Not only did God use words to bring forth all creation, He also passed the power of words on to us. And with that gift comes

great responsibility. Read the following verses and note the power we have been given through the gift of words.

Proverbs 18:21

Proverbs 21:23

Matthew 12:37

Revelation 12:11

5. I know of no better words than the ones inspired by God. When we ask, He will give us the words to say. Read Exodus 7:2. How did Moses know what to say to Pharaoh?

6. Read Jeremiah 1:17-19 and fill in the blanks below. Note: How did Jeremiah know what to say to the people of Israel?

" 'Get yourself ready! Stand up and _____ _____. Do not be terrified by them, or I will terrify you before them. Today I have made you _____, _____ and _____ to stand against the whole land— against the kings of Judah, its officials, its priests and the people of the land. They will fight against you but will not overcome you, for I am with you and will rescue you,' declares the LORD."

Jeremiah was a young prophet. What three word pictures did God use to describe the strength God had imparted to him?

1.

2.

3.

A fortified city was a symbol of security and impregnability. An iron pillar was a symbol of dignity and strength. A bronze wall was also a symbol of strength.* A bronze wall was used again to describe Jeremiah in Jeremiah 15:20. Where did that strength come from?

I believe that when we learn how to say the words that God would have us say, we will be a fortified city, an iron pillar, and a bronze wall—women of security, dignity, and strength.

7. Jesus told His disciples not to worry about the words they were to say if they were arrested for being Christians. What was His promise to them? Luke 12:11-12

8. Like Father, like Son. Let's look at what Jesus had to say about the power of words. How did He use His words in the following verses?

Matthew 8:24-27

Mark 9:25

---

* Kenneth Barker, general editor, *NIV Study Bible* (Grand Rapids, MI: Zondervan Publishing House, 1995), p. 1114.

Mark 11:12-14,20-24

Luke 7:14-15

9. Read and record Matthew 17:20.

In your own words, describe the potential of faith-filled words.

Rather than talk *about* our problems, Jesus was telling us to talk *to* our problems. Is there a mountain in your life that you need to speak to? If so, what do you need to say to it?

10. How was the power of God displayed through the words of Jesus' followers?

Acts 3:1-8

Acts 14:8-10

Acts 16:16-18

11. We have seen the power of God's words to create something out of nothing, the power of Jesus' words to control the physical and spiritual realms, and the power of man's words to bring healing. Now let's look at the importance of our words to bring new life spiritually. Read the following verses and note the importance of our words in redemption and healing.

   Romans 10:9-10

   James 5:16

   1 John 1:9

12. Read Matthew 16:15-19. What was Jesus' reaction to Peter's confession?

   What was Peter's reward?

13. Look up and define the word "confess." Does the definition add any insight into the verses above?

14. There is power in our confession of faith, and God does not want us to miss the blessing. Jesus could have chosen to quietly go

about healing the sick, but He wanted more for His followers. He wanted them to confess their faith with their mouths. Read Luke 8:43-48.

What was the woman's problem?

What happened when she touched Jesus' robe?

How was her touching Jesus' robe different from the multitudes pressing around Him?

Why do you think Jesus asked, "Who touched me?" What did He want the woman to do?

There is power in confession. God wants us to tell our stories (Revelation 12:11).

15. Jesus had another encounter with a woman who desired healing, but this healing was not for herself. It was for her daughter.

Read Matthew 15:21-28 and then describe the scene.

When Jesus used the word "dog," He was implying that the gospel was first intended for the Jews (lost sheep of Israel) rather than the Gentiles (dogs). She understood exactly what He meant as Gentiles were often referred to as such.

I do not believe that Jesus was speaking down to this woman. His response to her drew out the condition of her heart, and that served as an example of humility and faith to the disciples and to you and me.

What was the woman's response to Jesus in verse 27?

Would you describe her response as prideful or humble? Fearful or faithful?

What was the outcome of her humble faith-filled words?

Suppose she had responded with prideful words such as, "That's not fair" or "I deserve favor too." What do you think would have been the outcome?

16. Prior to this event, Jesus had engaged in a debate with the prideful Pharisees. The blackness of their hearts serves as a backdrop on which this woman's luminous humility shines. This same account is recorded in Mark 7:24-30. Mark reveals another aspect of her humble approach to Jesus. How did she address Jesus?

This was the only time Mark recorded someone addressing Jesus as Lord. What does this imply about her view of Jesus and the power of her confession?

17. Read Matthew 12:37 and fill in the blanks. "_____ _____ you will be acquitted, and by your words you will be condemned."

How does this verse reflect the truths we have learned about the power of words that come out of our mouths thus far?

18. Now for a little fun. In the first lesson we met a talking donkey. Now let's take a look at a scene that reads as though it were a script from a Hollywood movie. Ezekiel was a prophet who lived during one of the many times in the Old Testament when Israel rebelled against God. They resembled a dead dry nation. Read Ezekiel 37:1-10 and answer the following questions.

What did Ezekiel see in this vision?

What did God ask him to do?

What occurred when Ezekiel prophesied to the dead bones?

Just for fun, try your hand at drawing a series of pictures depicting these scenes. If you are doing this study in a group, share your frames. This is one instance where stick figures work best!

19. On a more serious note, is there some area of your life that seems hopeless—like a pile of dead dry bones? A marriage? A rebellious child? A financial struggle? Let me ask you, if God can take a pile of dried dead bones and make them into a powerful army, do you think He can take your seemingly hopeless situation and transform it?

    Take this opportunity to speak to those dry bones in a prayer to God.

    Dear Lord,

20. It is not enough just to speak words of faith. We must believe. Read and record 2 Corinthians 4:13. How does this verse relate what we believe to what we speak?

Do you see a connection between 2 Corinthians 4:13 and Ezekiel 37:1-10?

21. We speak words of faith, but God does the work to bring life. After the bones were resurrected, what did God do? Go back to Ezekiel 37:9-10 for your answer.

22. Yes, there is power in the words we speak, but we must always remember that God is sovereign, and He will do as He pleases. His actions will always be for our good (Romans 8:28). He may not always give us what we want, but He will always give us what we need. I am so glad God allows us to participate in His work, aren't you?

23. Summarize what you have learned today about the power of words.

A *W*OMAN'S *A*MAZING *P*OTENTIAL

Power verse:
*"Death and life are in the power of the tongue,
and those who love it will eat its fruit."*
PROVERBS 18:21 NASB

ALL THROUGH THE BIBLE we see men and women who encouraged and discouraged those around them. In this lesson we'll look at both.

1. Poor Job. He really had it rough. He lost his all his children, his herds and servants, and even his health. It seems the only thing he was left with was his contentious wife. Read Job 2:9. What was Mrs. Job's advice to her husband?

   Was she encouraging or discouraging?

2. Mary knew that her Son Jesus was special from the very beginning. Don't you just know she was anxious to see how His

life would affect the world? Read John 2:1-11. How did she encourage Jesus?

What was Jesus' response?

I don't think Jesus was disrespectful in the least. I imagine He had a twinkle in His eye as He toyed with His mom. Do you think Mary's request was encouragement to Jesus? Why or why not?

How did her words show that she believed in Him?

3. It's easy to pour cold water on someone's dreams or ministry. Read Acts 18:24-28. How did Priscilla and Aquila encourage rather than discourage Apollos?

Someone less sensitive to the Holy Spirit could have handled the situation differently. What might have been the outcome had Priscilla and Aquila harshly chastised Apollos rather than lovingly taught him?

Have you experienced both harsh chastisement and loving correction? If so, explain.

Which was more effective?

4. How does Paul recommend that we approach someone who needs correcting? Galatians 6:1

5. Ahab was a wicked king whose badness was surpassed only by his evil wife, Jezebel. Elijah was God's prophet during this time and came head-to-head with this conniving woman. Read 1 Kings 18:1-40 and describe the scene.

Was Elijah a confident man? On a scale of 1-10 (10 being the highest), where would you rate his faith?

1   2   3   4   5   6   7   8   9   10

6. Let's look at the next miracle. Read 1 Kings 18:41-46 and describe what God did next.

7. Jezebel was furious because of the miracles of Elijah and his God. What was her response to Elijah? 1 Kings 19:1-2

8. How did this mighty man of God, this rock of faith, respond to Jezebel's threats? 1 Kings 19:3-5

9. Stop the mental video and push "pause" on the frame of Elijah sleeping under the broom tree. What strikes you as odd about his response to Jezebel's threats?

Are you amazed at the power of this woman's words over this mighty man of faith?

10. While nothing surprises God, I believe even He was amazed at this sudden sinking faith. What did He ask Elijah? 1 Kings 19:9,13

11. I think this was a question to make Elijah think and bring him back to his senses. If we ever get off track because someone's words have discouraged us or extinguished our hope, God gives us the way to return. "Go back the way you came" (1 Kings 19:15). Have you ever felt that God was telling you to go back the way you came? If so, explain.

There have been times in my life when I have realized that I am way off track of where I wanted to be. One of the best ways I know to get back on track is to mentally walk back through the days and figure out where I made a wrong turn. That is what

God instructed Elijah to do. Afterward, Elijah came out of the cave of despair and got back onto the path of peace.

12. Summarize what you have learned about the power of one woman's words to extinguish the hopes and dreams of another.

13. We've seen how a woman's words have the potential to encourage someone to fulfill God's call on his life and the potential to get someone off track from accomplishing what God has called him to do. Now let's look at how the words of a woman prevented a man from straying from God's will and making a terrible mistake.

Read 1 Samuel 25 and answer the following questions.

How was Abigail described?

How was her husband described?

It may seem odd for us to imagine such an intelligent woman marrying such a wicked man, but in those days, most marriages were arranged. It's possible she had very little to do with the choice of her husband.

14. David had been appointed to succeed King Saul, but at this point in history he was hiding in the wilderness because Saul was attempting to take his life. While hiding, David and his men had been protecting Nabal's sheep. It seemed only right

for Nabal to be grateful for David's assistance and protection. However, what was Nabal's answer to David's request for provisions?

How did David respond?

15. Abigail was a wise woman. She wasted no time once she heard that David and his men were on their way to slaughter her household. She not only gathered provisions but also used her words to defuse David's anger.

What did she say to calm David down and bring him to his senses?

Was her posture one of pride or humility?

Notice how she gently reminded David of who he was as a child of God.

16. God took care of Nabal. David didn't have to. We never need to use our words or actions for revenge. What does Paul tell us about taking vengeance into our own hands? Romans 12:19

How can we be like the wise Abigail when it comes to defusing someone's anger?

17. Read and record Proverbs 15:1.

    Give an example of how you have seen that played out in your own life.

18. Let's look at another mighty man of God, Peter.

    First, let's rate Peter on the faith-o-meter. Read the following verses and rate Peter's faith. Matthew 16:15-17; Luke 22:31-33

    1   2   3   4   5   6   7   8   9   10

19. Now read Matthew 26:69-75. What words came out of Peter's mouth to prove that he was not a follower of Christ to the servant girl?

    What does that tell you about the perception of cursing to those who listen?

20. It is amazing that we can encourage someone's dream at one moment and then say words that discourage them the next. Michal was a woman who started out being her husband's chief cheerleader, but she ended up being his chief critic. Read 1 Samuel 19:11-17. How did Michal encourage and protect her husband?

21. For many years, the Ark of the Covenant had been in enemy hands. However, King David conquered his enemies and brought the ark back to God's people where it belonged. It was his dream come true. Read 2 Samuel 6:16-23 to get a glimpse of David's elation.

    How did David show an outward display of praise to God?

    What was Michal's response to David's praise?

    Was she attempting to encourage or extinguish his dreams?

    What was the result of her disdain?

22. Have you ever put a damper on someone's enthusiasm? If so, how could you have handled the situation differently?

    How do you encourage your husband in his relationship with God?

23. God is our ultimate example of how to use our words to encourage the hopes and dreams of those around us. Read the following verses and note how God encouraged His servants to do what He had called them to do.

Joshua 1:1-9

Judges 6:11-16 (Note that Gideon was threshing wheat in a winepress. Wheat was usually threshed in an open field. Gideon was hiding!)

Jeremiah 1:4-19

24. God has plans for His children. Read and note what the following verses say about the plans He has for us.

Jeremiah 29:11

1 Corinthians 2:9

Ephesians 2:10

25. Dear friend, could it be that our discouraging words would keep someone from attempting the dreams God has for her? Could it be that our words could bolster someone's faith and give her the courage to accomplish all that God has called her to do? Yes, we have great power and potential in our words. Have you ever

had someone try to extinguish your dreams with her words? If so, explain.

Have you ever had someone encourage your dreams with her words? If so, explain.

(These would be excellent answers to share with the group.)

26. Make a list of ways you can use your words to encourage someone's dream.

THE POWER OF A WOMAN'S WORDS TO HER CHILDREN

Power verse:

*"Train up a child in the way he should go,
and when he is old he will not turn from it."*

PROVERBS 22:6

FROM THE TIME A CHILD IS BORN, parents are given a very brief period in which to shape and mold an eternal soul. God has given us the privilege of impacting the children who will one day define who we are as a community and a nation. And we do that primarily with the words we speak.

1. Read the following and note how Jesus felt about children.

Matthew 19:13-14

Mark 9:36-37

Mark 9:42

2. Today we are going to delve into the life of one man to discover the effects his mother's words had on his life and his character. We will be skimming Genesis 25–32, but stopping along the way to ponder a few of the scenes. Read Genesis 25:19-34 and answer the following questions.

    What did God tell Rebekah about her children? (verse 23)

    "The _____ will serve the _____."

    Who was older?

    Who was younger?

    Write their names above the words you wrote in the blanks.

3. Give a brief description of the two boys.

    Esau:

    Jacob:

4. Now let's fast forward to Genesis 27. Describe the setting:

    What did Rebekah instruct Jacob to do? Record verse 8.

What role did Rebekah play in the deception?

5. Does anything jump out at you in 27:20? Whom did Jacob bring into the picture?

6. Take a close look at Genesis 27:8 and fill in the blanks:

"Now, my son, _____

and _____."

Similar words appear in 27:43. What did she say?

7. Have you ever said those words to your child?

8. What does Rebekah teach us about the impact "do what I say" has on a child?

9. Rebekah interfered with God's plan and taught her younger son to lie. Do you remember what God told her about her children before they were born? Was her interference necessary to accomplish what God had already promised?

Do you think He could have accomplished what He had planned without her meddling? Read Isaiah 14:27 for further insight.

10. Jacob stole a blessing that God would have freely given. We don't know how God would have fulfilled His promise, but we know He always does. Read the following verses for further insight.

Joshua 23:14

Jeremiah 1:12

Ezekiel 12:28

11. Jacob's mother was a schemer, trickster, and deceiver. By her words she passed on her uncanny ability to her son. Jacob fled his father's house and ran from his brother, Esau, who threatened to kill him. He settled in Paddan Aram and married two sisters. Just for fun, skim Genesis 29 and note how Laban tricked the trickster.

12. Now let's pick back up on the story in Genesis 30:25–31:20. Jacob was planning on leaving his father-in-law and returning to his homeland. What trick did he play on his father-in-law?

Where do you think he learned his deceptive ways?

I don't understand Jacob's use of the peeled polar branches to influence the birth of the sheep. I suspect that the sticks had very little to do with the genetic properties of the sheep. However, it does show that Jacob was still trying to use trickery rather than depending on God's blessing.

13. God had a plan for Jacob, but first he had to change his deceiving ways passed on to him by his mother. Read Genesis 32:22-32.

    Who do you think this man was whom Jacob wrestled?

    What did Jacob ask the stranger to do?

    Why do you think Jacob still did not feel blessed, even though he had already received his father's blessing in chapter 27?

14. What did the stranger ask Jacob in Genesis 32:27?

    When Jacob had tricked his father into blessing him, what had his father asked? Genesis 27:18

    What was Jacob's reply to his father?

    What was Jacob's reply to God's representative? Genesis 32:27

15. God changed Jacob's name from _____ to
    _____. No longer was he to be known as Jacob,
    which means "trickster," but Israel.

16. The good news is that Jacob did learn his lesson. Read the fol-
    lowing verses about when he blessed his grandsons in Genesis
    48:12-20.

    What did Jacob do during the blessing?

    How does this differ from the way he had been taught by his
    mother's deceptive words?

    Friend, we never need to pretend to be someone we are not in
    order to receive a blessing. We may try to look like, sound like,
    smell like, and feel like someone else, but it is not necessary. It
    is detrimental. And what about a mother's words to her chil-
    dren? We never need to use our words to try to manipulate our
    children to look like, sound like, smell like, or feel like someone
    other than who God created them to be. God has a specific plan
    for each one of them (Jeremiah 29:11). He created them for a
    unique purpose. Our role is to guide them along the path that
    God has chosen all along.

17. Summarize what you have learned from the story of Rebekah
    and how her words affected her son.

18. What are some ways a mother's words teach her children to be deceptive? For example:

    The phone rings and she says to little Johnny, "Tell them I'm not at home."

    The family wants to take a long weekend to go to the beach. She tells little Sarah, "We'll just write a note to your teacher and tell her you are sick."

    What are some other possible scenarios that teach children how to lie?

    1.

    2.

    3.

    4.

19. A mother's words to her children will have lasting effects. Where did Timothy first learn about Jesus? 2 Timothy 1:5

20. I want you to imagine someone writing a letter to your child similar to the one Paul wrote to Timothy. How would you like to be remembered? Fill in your "dream" letter.

    Dear _____, I want you to remember what you have learned from your mother's faith in Christ.

Remember how she taught you _____

_____

_____.

Remember what you learned from her example. _____

_____

_____.

Remember the words she spoke to you about Jesus _____

_____

_____.

21. Whether we realize it or not, our children are watching and listening to our actions and words. What did Paul say to his spiritual children in Philippians 3:17?

    Would you tell your children to follow your example in how they speak to others?

22. No parent can be a perfect parent, but every parent can be a praying parent. We are going to concentrate on prayer more in lesson 9, but I can think of no better way to end this lesson on the power of a woman's words to her children than using our words in the most powerful way possible, in prayer. You, too, can pray that your children will:

    • Know Christ as Savior early in life. (2 Timothy 3:15)

    • Have a hatred for sin. (Psalm 97:10)

    • Be caught when guilty. (Psalm 119:71)

- Be protected from the evil one in each area of their lives: spiritual, emotional, and physical. (John 17:15)

- Have a responsible attitude in all their interpersonal relationships. (Daniel 6:3)

- Respect those in authority over them. (Romans 13:1)

- Desire the right kind of friends and be protected from the wrong friends. (Proverbs 1:10-11)

- Be kept from the wrong mate and saved for the right one. (2 Corinthians 6:14-17)

- Be kept pure until marriage (as well as the one they marry). (1 Corinthians 6:18-20)

- Learn to totally submit to God and actively resist Satan in all things. (James 4:7)

- Be single-hearted, willing to be sold out to Jesus Christ. (Romans 12:1-2)

- Be hedged in so they cannot find their way to wrong people or wrong places and that the wrong people cannot find their way to them. (Hosea 2:6)

I keep a laminated prayer card in my Bible to remind me to pray Scripture over my child. He is now a young adult, and even though the frayed card has been replaced many times with new ones, the powerful words of Scripture that pass from my lips to God are as powerful as the day they were penned more than 2000 years ago.*

---

* For information on ordering laminated Scripture prayer cards, visit www.sharonjaynes.com.

The Power of a Woman's Words to Her Husband

Power verse:

"An excellent wife, who can find?
For her worth is far above jewels."

PROVERBS 31:10 NASB

IN THE LAST LESSON we took an in-depth look at one mother in the Bible and how her words affected her son. Now let's delve into Scripture and take a close look at how the words of a woman affected her husband. The woman's name is Sarai—the wife of Abram.

1. For background, read Genesis 11:26-32.

   Who was Sarai?

   What was her condition?

   Terah took his family and headed out for Canaan. But the caravan never made it to their destination. Read Genesis 11:31 and fill in the blanks.

"Terah took his son Abram, his grandson Lot son of Haran, and his daughter-in-law, Sarai, the wife of his son Abram, and together they set out from Ur of the Chaldeans to go to _____. But when they came to Haran, they _____ there."

Canaan is often referred to as the Promised Land (Genesis 17:8; 50:24; Exodus 33:1). I live in North Carolina. A similar comparison of distance would be if I were to set out on a journey to Texas, but I stopped in Tennessee and settled there.

Look up and define the word "settle."

I hope you discovered that "settle" can have two meanings. It means to take up permanent residence or it can mean to not hold out for something better. How could both definitions fit Genesis 11:31?

2. Read Genesis 12:1-3 and fill in the blanks.

"_____ make you into a great nation and _____ bless you. _____ make your name great and you will be a blessing. _____ bless those who bless you, and whoever curses you _____ curse and all of the peoples on earth will be blessed through you."

Skip down to verse 7 and fill in the blank.

"The LORD appeared to Abram and said, 'To your offspring _____ give this land.'"

Let's summarize what we have learned so far. Who was going to bless Abram and future generations through him?

3. A lot transpired between Genesis chapters 12 and 15. I encourage you to go back and read those chapters at a later time. But for now let's just know that many years passed and Sarai still did not have a son.

    What does God say to reaffirm His promise to Abram in Genesis 15:1-6?

    Fill in the blank of this very important verse, Genesis 15:6.

    "Abram _____ the LORD and he credited it to him as righteousness."

4. What does all this have to do with the power of a woman's words? We're getting there. First we needed to establish the strength of Abram's faith. On a scale of 1 to 10, 10 being the highest, how would you rate Abram's faith and trust in God? Circle it below.

    1   2   3   4   5   6   7   8   9   10

5. We haven't heard much from Sarai. We can assume she has been somewhat cooperative in pulling up stakes and moving to only God knew where. But when it came to waiting on God to provide Abram an heir, it seems her faith didn't match that of her righteous husband. Read Genesis 16:1-2. What did Sarai suggest to Abram?

   This may seem very strange to us in our modern culture, but providing an heir through a servant was an ancient custom to ensure the birth of a male heir. Do you see any similarities between Sarai and Rebekah from lesson 4?

   Looking back at what you just wrote, pick one word to describe them.

6. Let's go back to Genesis 11:31.

   "But when they came to Haran, they _____ there."

   What was Sarai asking Abram to do in Genesis 16:1-2?

   Have you ever *settled* for less than what God had promised?

   Have you ever suggested that someone *settle* for less than what they believed God had promised to them?

7. Go back to Genesis 16 and read verses 1-6.

   What was the outcome of Abram following Sarai's suggestion?

   Describe Sarai's response to Abram once Hagar was pregnant.

   Whom did she blame for her unhappiness?

8. Sarai isn't the only woman in Scripture who used her words to
   make her husband feel guilty for something that was not his
   fault. Read Genesis 39:1-18. Whom did Potiphar's wife ultimately blame?

   Oh, my. Have you ever interfered with God's plans and then
   blamed the blundering outcome on someone else? If so, and if
   you are brave enough to admit it, record the incident.

9. Abram and Sarai's saga continues. Turn back to Genesis 17:1-8.
   Remember, we're focusing on the power of a woman's words on
   her husband. But, friend, these are some of my favorite passages
   in Scripture. They are rich with lessons on the sovereignty of
   God and His faithfulness to us when we are unfaithful to Him.
   You will be blessed if you read straight through from Genesis
   12–14, but for now let's stick to the lesson at hand…Genesis
   17:1-8. Abram was 75 when God first spoke to him. How many
   years have passed when we come on the scene in chapter 17?

Summarize God's renewed covenant in your own words.

10. Note that God changed Abram's name to _____. In verse
15, God changed Sarai's name to _____. Abram means
"exalted father," most likely a reference to God being the Exalted
Father. Abraham means "father of many," pointing to Abraham
being the father of many nations. In the Hebrew language, both
names, Sarai and Sarah, mean "princess." God emphasized in
these verses that she was going to become the mother of nations
and kings would come from her. The name changes may seem
small and insignificant to us, but when God changed someone's
name, He marked them in a special way as His servant.

11. Let's pick up the story in Genesis 18:10-15.

How old was Sarah when she heard the angel's prophecy?

What was her response?

Can't you just see the scene?

    "You laughed!"
    "Did not."
    "Did too."

Laugh or no laugh, verse 14 is no laughing matter. This is just too good to pass up. What was the angel's response to Sarah's laughter? Record Genesis 18:14 and memorize it this week!

12. Turn the pages and read Genesis 21:1-5. (Don't you just love the sound of the rustling of the pages of God's Word? He does. It is music to His ears.)

How did God fulfill His promise to Abraham?

How old was Abraham?

Sarah was ten years younger than Abraham. How old was she when was Isaac was born?

13. I don't know how you rated Abraham's faith, but I'm guessing it was fairly high. Were you amazed that the words of his beautiful wife could cause such a strong faith to waver?

Read Genesis 3:6 and compare Adam's response to Eve and Abram's response to Sarai. How are they similar?

Does that leave you shaking in your boots, or bedroom slippers, or whatever you have on at the moment?

14. As we sum up the story of Abraham and Sarah to the point of Isaac's birth, what insight have you gleaned into the power of a woman's words to her husband?

15. The book of Proverbs has much wisdom and insight into the potential of a woman's words. Read the following proverbs and note the contrast between a woman who uses her words well and the woman who uses her words poorly.

Proverbs 12:4

Proverbs 19:13

Proverbs 19:14

Proverbs 21:19

Proverbs 25:24

Proverbs 31:10,26,28,29

Which verses describe you best?

16. By the way, whatever happened to Ishmael, the son born to Abraham through Sarah's servant Hagar? He became the father of the Arab nation, just as Isaac became the father of the Jewish

nation. In light of the Arab/Jewish conflict that has raged and continues to rage today, ponder the long-lasting affects of Sarah's interference.

Will you make a commitment with me to only use your words to strengthen your husband's faith and not cause him to settle for anything other than God's best for his life? If so, pray the following prayer with me and fill in the blank with your husband's name.

Heavenly Father. I thank You so much for _____.
He is a precious gift to me. I pray that I will always use my words
to strengthen his faith. I commit to never use my words
to manipulate him to do what I want him to do rather than what
You have called him to do. Help me to be a woman who helps my
husband be all You have called him to be. Please convict me,
by the power of the Holy Spirit, if I am ever causing his faith
in You to waver. And, Lord, please help me not to interfere with
Your divine plans. In Jesus' name, amen.

*Th*e *P*ower of a *W*oman's *W*ords to *H*er *F*riends

Power verse:

*"The heartfelt counsel of a friend is as
sweet as perfume and incense."*

PROVERBS 27:9 NLT

PERHAPS SOME OF THE EASIEST PEOPLE to give encouraging words to
are our friends. We don't get to choose our family, but we do get
to choose our friends. Someone once said, "The best way to have a
friend is to be one." Let's see what the Bible teaches about how to
use our words to bless and benefit our friends.

1. We use our words to encourage our friends, but what exactly is
    encouragement? My dictionary defines "encourage" this way:
    "to give courage, spirit, or hope; to stimulate." Look up each of
    those descriptive words for greater insight.

    Courage:

    Spirit:

Hope:

Stimulate:

With the added knowledge of these definitions, write an expanded definition of the words "encourage" and "encouragement."

2. What part do words play in encouragement?

3. What do the following verses teach about the importance of encouragement?

Deuteronomy 1:38; 3:28

2 Samuel 19:7

Isaiah 1:17

Acts 15:32

Ephesians 6:22

1 Thessalonians 4:18

Looking back at the four aspects of the word "encourage," note which you see demonstrated in each of the previous verses.

4. Hebrews 10:17-25 gives us the foundational reason for encouraging our friends. Let's look at these verses closely. Read and record the action verbs or action statements found in Hebrews 10:17-25.

   The word "consider" in verse 24 means "to observe fully; behold, discover, perceive." What does this definition reveal about the time and effort that is involved in true encouragement?

   The Greek for "spur" in verse 24 means to "sharpen alongside." What does Proverbs 27:17 teach about our ability to sharpen?

   What does the word "alongside" imply?

5. Jesus could have easily come to earth and lived in solitude. Instead, He chose to live in relationship with others. He ministered to the multitudes, but He had 12 close friends. Read the following verses and note how Jesus needed His friends' support during His last days on earth.

Matthew 26:36-46

Mark 14:32-42

Luke 22:39-46

6. Not only did Jesus need the encouragement of His friends, He knew they needed and would need His words of encouragement as well. Scan the following passages and give each one a title.

Luke 9:1-6

Jesus encourages His disciples by _____.

John 4:1-26

Jesus encourages the woman at the well by _____.

John 14:8-14

Jesus encourages Phillip by _____.

John 17:20-26; Romans 8:34

Jesus encourages you by _____.

John 20:24-29

Jesus encourages Thomas by _____.

John 21:15-19

Jesus encourages Peter by _____.

7. What was David's dilemma in Psalm 55:12-14?

Why are the hurtful words of a friend most painful?

8. Poor Job. We have looked at his plight several times, but today let's focus on the words of his friends. Read Job 2:11-13. List at least three ways Job's friends showed genuine compassion for him.

    1.

    2.

    3.

The best thing they did was sit in silence. It wasn't until they opened their mouths that compassion and consolation evaporated like the morning fog.

Scan the following verses and note the words of Job's friends.

Job 4:7-8

Job 8:4,20

Job 11:5-7

Read Job 16:1-5. What did Job tell them about their words?

In other words: Thanks but no thanks.

9. Read and record Galatians 6:2.

How can we help "carry each other's burdens" with the words we speak?

10. Read the following proverbs and note the effect of a good word to a friend.

Proverbs 10:11

Proverbs 12:25

Proverbs 15:23

Proverbs 15:30

Proverbs 16:24

Proverbs 25:11

Proverbs 25:25

11. How did the following women use their words to encourage their friends?

Ruth to Naomi: Ruth 1:16-17

Elizabeth to Mary: Luke 1:39-45

The misuse of words can destroy a friendship. There are many abuses of the tongue that shatter relationships between friends, but let's look at just three: gossip, slander, and deceit.

12. GOSSIP

Look up and record the definition of the word "gossip" in the dictionary.

My dictionary used the words "habitually repeats intimate or private rumors as fact." Gossip is a verb and a noun. In other words, you can participate in gossip or be a gossip.

13. Read Romans 1:28-32 and fill in the blanks.

"Furthermore, since they did not think it worthwhile to retain the knowledge of God, he gave them over to a depraved mind, to do what ought not to be done. They have become filled with every kind of wickedness, evil, greed and depravity. They are full of envy, murder, strife, deceit and malice. They are_____, _____, God-haters, insolent, arrogant and boastful; they invent ways of doing evil; they disobey their parents; they are senseless, faithless, heartless, ruthless. Although they know God's righteous decree that those who do such things deserve death, they not only continue to do these very things but also _____ of those who practice them."

Were you surprised that gossip and slander were smack-dab in the middle of such depravity?

What does that tell you about the gravity of our words?

14. What do the following verses teach about gossip?

Proverbs 16:28

2 Corinthians 12:20

1 Timothy 5:13

15. What does our culture think of gossip?

     Think about how many publications and television programs would be eliminated if gossip were outlawed. Jot down just a few.

     1.

     2.

     3.

     4.

     5.

16. Why do you think gossip is so attractive?

17. The pull to gossip is so strong that unless we resolve to abstain from it, we probably will gossip. Write down some ways that you can prevent yourself from doing so.

18. **SLANDER**

     Slander is very similar to gossip. Look up "slander" in the dictionary and record your findings.

     How are slander and gossip similar?

How are slander and gossip different?

19. Read the following verses and note what the Bible teaches about the dangers of slander.

Psalm 101:5

Proverbs 10:18

Titus 3:1-2

20. Has anyone ever said something to mar your reputation?

21. What does Proverbs 22:1 say about the importance of a person's reputation?

22. I doubt that many people would say that slander is acceptable behavior. However, it is still widely practiced. How does the world disguise slander to make it appear acceptable and financially profitable? (Example: Gossip magazines.)

23. DECEIT

Deceit is another use of words that destroys friendships. Read Proverbs 20:23. How does God feel about dishonesty?

24. Deceit and dishonesty both involve misleading or concealing the truth. How is Satan described in John 8:44? What is his native language?

So when we lie, we are speaking Satanese.

25. How is Jesus described in the following verses?

John 1:14

John 14:6

Jesus said, "I tell you the truth…" more than 80 times in the New Testament. Truth is important to God because it is His very nature. Likewise, as we have seen, deception is Satan's very nature. It is who he is and what he does.

26. To emphasis just how devastating the effects of deception are, read Genesis 3:4-5. What did Satan tell Eve?

I hope you wrote down that he told her a lie. Actually, it was the first lie in the Bible! Just think. It was a lie, deception, dishonesty, that caused the fall of mankind and ushered sin and death into the world. No wonder God hates lies.

27. Now, read 1 John 3:8. Why did Jesus come into the world?

28. Honesty does not mean we tell everyone everything. We must still be women of discretion who speak words of grace. However, honesty does mean that we will never mislead anyone with a lie or deceit. Will you commit with me to let truth be the guiding principle of the words you speak? When you speak truth, you are speaking the native language of your heavenly Father.

29. As long as we have a mouth, we will be tempted to use our words in hurtful ways. However, what is the promise of 1 Corinthians 10:13?

    (A simple solution is found in Job 40:4.)

30. Most know the Golden Rule: "Do to others as you would have them do to you." However, many do not know that it actually came from the Bible (Luke 6:31). In closing I want you to do a simple exercise. Write down ten things you would like for a friend to do to encourage you. Then write down ten kind words you would like to hear. I'll get you started.

Ten things I would like a friend to do to encourage me.

1. Send me a card.

2.

3.

4.

5.

6.

7.

8.

9.

10.

Ten words I would love to hear from a friend.

1. Thank you for being such a good friend.

2.

3.

4.

5.

6.

7.

8.

9.

10.

Now let's go back to the Golden Rule. Over the next ten weeks, do for someone else what you desire for someone to do for you. Send a card with encouraging words. Tell someone why her friendship is so valuable to you. Go ahead. Get started. You'll be amazed at the rich rewards of blessing a friend with your very words!

The Power of a Woman's Words to Fellow Believers

Power verse:

"Be mindful to be a blessing, especially to those of the household of faith, those who belong to God's family with you, the believers."

GALATIANS 6:10 AMP

IT'S EASY TO FEEL INSIGNIFICANT in the large body of Christ. Perhaps we think, *How can my simple words encourage the church?* Let's look at one little woman whose words had a big effect.

1. Read Luke 2:36-38.

Who was Anna?

How long had she been married?

How long had she been widowed?

How did Anna spend her days?

How did Anna encourage Mary and Joseph at this crucial moment of their lives?

I imagine that Anna felt her existence as an elderly poor widow was not very significant. And yet she was memorialized in God's Word for her words of encouragement to Mary and Joseph during one of the most important, and I imagine, confusing times of their lives. What does this teach you about the power of seemingly insignificant words that you speak to a fellow believer?

2. God did not intend for believers to live in isolation. Even in the Old Testament, when He established the Jews as His chosen people, He called them to live in community. Look up and define the word "community." What makes a group of people a community?

3. Read the following verses and note how God called His people to live in community.

Genesis 28:3

Exodus 12:47

Exodus 16:1-2,9-10,22

Jeremiah 30:19-20,22

4. God called the nation of Israel to live in community with each other...acting as one. In the New Testament, we see that same intention with followers of Christ. Read Hebrews 10:19-25. There are five exhortations that include the words, "Let us..." Summarize the exhortations below.

   Verse 22:

   Verse 23:

   Verse 24:

   Verse 25:

   Verse 25:

   Which of those involve the words we speak?

5. The Greek word translated "spur" (verse 24) in the NIV is *paroxuno*, which means "to sharpen alongside." From what you have

learned thus far in this study, how can your words "sharpen" a
fellow believer to reach his or her God-given potential?

How can your words "dull" a fellow believer or render him or
her ineffective?

Notice the Greek word "spur" means to sharpen alongside. We
looked at this in the previous lesson. As a reminder, what does
the word "alongside" imply?

6. In the Bible, there are many examples of men and women who
    encouraged one another in their faith. Look up the following
    verses and note the words spoken.

    Deuteronomy 3:28: Moses encouraged _____.

    Acts 15:32: Judas and Silas encouraged _____.

    2 Corinthians 7:6: Titus encouraged _____.

    Ephesians 6:21-22: Tychicus encouraged _____.

7. One man named Joseph was such an encourager, the apostles changed his name. Read Acts 4:36. To what did they change his name?

His name meant "son of encouragement." Wouldn't it be wonderful if we became so encouraging among fellow believers that our names were changed to Daughters of Encouragement?

8. How often are we to encourage one another? Hebrews 3:13

While we cannot be everywhere at once to encourage fellow believers, we can be the cheerleader to the ones we speak to on any given day. Also, we can pray. I know of no better way to be an encourager in the body of Christ.

9. Did you know there could be competition in the body of Christ? It pains me to say it, but envy and competition are two stumbling blocks in the church that keep men and women from being the encouragers God intended.

Read Matthew 27:18. Why did the chief priests hand Jesus over to Pilate?

Read Luke 9:46-48. What were the disciples arguing about?

What was Jesus' reply?

10. John the Baptist is a wonderful example of the noncompetitive spirit that we are to have among believers. When his followers came to him and told him that Jesus' followers were outnumbering his own, what was John's reply? John 3:27-30, especially verse 30.

11. God does not want us to compete against our brothers and sisters in Christ. Rather, He calls us to think of others as more important than ourselves and to help others accomplish their dreams. What are some ways you can help fellow believers accomplish their dreams?

   Write down the names of five Christians you could encourage over the next week.

   1.

   2.

   3.

   4.

   5.

12. Read Colossians 3:12-17. How are we to clothe ourselves?

   1.

   2.

   3.

4.

5.

How do each of these articles of spiritual clothing affect the words we speak? Go back up to your list and note an example of each.

What is Paul's plumb line for our words mentioned in verse 17? Fill in the blank.

"And whatever you do, whether in _____ or deed, do it all in the name of the Lord Jesus, giving thanks to God the Father through him."

13. One reason it is so important for us to speak to fellow believers with an attitude of love is because that is how the world will know that there is something different about Christians. Read the following verses and note what you learn about the way we are to love one another. Also, take note of the reasons why we are to love each other openly.

John 13:34-35

John 15:12-13

1 John 3:10 (This verse gives me shivers as I think about the seriousness of loving fellow believers well with my words!)

1 John 3:11-12 (Note: This is an example of competitive attitude taken to the ultimate extreme.)

1 John 4:7-12

14. Unfortunately, many times when the world listens to the echoes of fellow believers in the world, they are not hearing people who love each other well.

Read Galatians 5:14 and fill in the blanks.

"The entire law is summed up in a single command: 'Love your neighbor as yourself.' If you keep on _____ and _____ each other, watch out or you will be _____ by each other."

The Greek word for "bite" is *dakno*. It means to "bite with the teeth." Metaphorically, to wound the soul, cut, lacerate. Now, obviously, they were not actually physically taking a bite out of each other. How do we bite each other with our words? Give some examples.

The Greek word for "devour" is *katesthio*. It means to "consume, eat up." Metaphorically, to devour, squander, waste, to strip one of his goods, to consume strength of body and mind by strong emotions. Considering the Greek definition, how do our words devour one another?

15. How do you think people who are not Christians interpret the backbiting and condemnation that goes on among believers?

Do you think that makes Christianity appealing?

That was a silly question, but I want us to ponder the idea that our words and how we treat each other in the body of Christ may push someone away or draw them closer to a personal relationship with Jesus. That is the power of a woman's words.

16. What did Jesus say about judging others in Matthew 7:1-5?

17. If you have children, how do you feel when someone talks badly about your son or daughter?

What are Christians called in the New Testament? John 1:12

So when we talk badly about a fellow believer, we are talking badly against one of God's children. How do you think your heavenly Father feels when we talk that way about one of His kids?

18. In chapter 7 of *The Power of a Woman's Words,* we read about

the Shunammite woman who encouraged the prophet Elisha by building a guest room onto her house for him. In return, Elisha prayed that God would bless her with a son. His prayers were answered and the Shunammite woman gave birth to her only child. Let's pick up the story a few years later to learn more about this woman's words of faith who encouraged a fellow believer. Read 2 Kings 4:18-37.

What happened to the boy?

How did she respond? (verses 23 and 26)

Where did she go for help?

Was she persistent or passive? Explain.

What was the outcome of this woman's words and acts of faith?

This was not the first time a son had been raised from the dead and it would not be the last! 1 Kings 17:17-24; John 20:1-9

19. One way that Paul encouraged fellow believers was through prayer. He didn't simply say, "I'll pray for you." He prayed! Read the following excerpt from his letter to the Ephesians and note what he prayed.

"For this reason I kneel before the Father, from whom his whole family in heaven and on earth derives its name. I pray that out of his glorious riches he may _____

_____

_____

in your inner being, so that Christ may dwell in your hearts through faith. And I pray that you, being _____

_____, may have _____,
together with all the saints, to grasp how wide and long and high and deep is the love of Christ, _____

_____—that you

may be _____

_____" (Ephesians 3:14-19).

If you had received those words in a letter from a friend, how would they have made you feel? Guess what. You have! Those words are written to you just as much as they were written to the members of the church at Ephesus. Consider writing such a prayer to one of your fellow travelers in the faith as a means of encouraging him or her today.

THE POWER OF A WOMAN'S WORDS TO THE WORLD

Power verse:

"We are therefore Christ's ambassadors, as though God were making His appeal through us."

2 CORINTHIANS 5:20

ARE YOU AWARE THAT everywhere you go today, people will be listening to what you say and watching how you act? For many, you and I are the only Bible they will read. Today, we're going to take a look at how God's children's words leave a lasting impression of the character of God Himself...be it true or false.

1. The people of Israel served as slaves to the Egyptians for 400 years. God freed them from slavery and sent them on a journey to the Promised Land of Canaan. But because of disobedience and a lack of faith, they wandered in the desert for 40 years. As we open the book of Joshua, God is about to take the Israelites across the Jordan River and into the land flowing with milk and honey. Read Joshua 2 and answer the following questions.

   Who was Rahab?

You may wonder why the spies chose the house of a prostitute. Jericho was a very busy city, and it was common for travelers to stay or visit such a place. By entering the house of a prostitute, they would appear to be just like every other traveler in the land.

2. What was Rahab's courageous act?

3. Let's focus on Rahab's words in verses 8-21. Complete the following.

    I know…

    We have heard…

    What was her profession of faith in verse 11? Be specific.

4. Rahab did not have a Bible, access to a church, or the Internet. She was dependent on what she heard others say. Thinking about your own life, do you think that someone would make such a profession of faith because of what they hear you say or see you do? I am sure they already have. Write a brief story of someone who was drawn to Christ because of listening to you.

5. What was the outcome of Rahab's profession of faith in God? Joshua 6:17-25

Rahab was even listed in Hebrews 11, the great Hall of Faith. Read and record Hebrews 11:31.

Not only does her faith line the halls of heaven as a portrait of trust and courage, she married an Israelite and became the great-great-grandmother of King David and was in the lineage of Jesus Christ.

6. From reading this amazing story, what can you surmise about the impact of your words for Christ as you go through your daily routine? How far-reaching is your influence?

7. Let's turn our attention to the impact our words have on the people we come in contact with every day. Read 2 Corinthians 2:14-15. What are we called?

Look up and define "fragrance."

8. Read John 12:3 and fill in the blanks.

"Then Mary took about a pint of pure nard, an expensive

perfume; she poured it on Jesus' feet and wiped his feet with her hair. And the _____

_____."

What happens when you walk into a room filled with smoke or stand in an elevator with a woman doused with heavy perfume?

9. The more time we spend with Jesus, the more we will carry His fragrance with us. How are your words like fragrance, good or bad?

10. Read 2 Corinthians 5:20. What are we called?

Define "ambassador." What is an ambassador's primary mission?

How important are an ambassador's words to the one they represent?

Would you say that you are representing King Jesus well with the words you speak?

11. Read Matthew 5:13. What does Jesus call you?

List three functions of salt.

1.

2.

3.

How can our words accomplish all three?

1.

2.

3.

12. One function of salt is for healing. Swimming in a salty sea heals a scraped knee, and being around salty Christians can heal a wounded soul. Let's look at a "salty" servant and see how she aided in the healing of her master. Read 2 Kings 5:1-14 and answer the following questions.

Who was Naaman?

What was his problem?

Who knew the source of healing for Naaman?

Do you think it took courage for her to offer the solution? Why or why not?

What was the outcome of this servant girl being salt to this Gentile man?

How can our words bring the ultimate healing to a hurting world?

13. Read Colossians 4:5-6 and fill in the blanks.

"Be _____ in the way you act toward outsiders; make the most of every opportunity. Let your conversation be always _____,
_____ so that you may know how to answer everyone."

We have already looked at what it means to have words seasoned with salt. Now let's look at the word "grace." If our words should be full of grace, then we need to make sure we know what grace sounds like. Look up and define "grace."

Rewrite the definition in your own words.

14. The Greek word for "grace" is *charis*. It is where we get the word "charity." God's greatest act of grace is the free gift of salvation through His Son, Jesus Christ. While we may think of charity

as something we do, how can we think of charity as something we say?

15. How is God described in 1 Peter 5:10?

16. What do the following verses tell us about God's grace?

    Romans 5:15

    2 Corinthians 9:14

    2 Corinthians 12:9

    Ephesians 1:6

    Ephesians 2:7

    Now go back up to each of those descriptions of God's grace and apply them to our speech. How can our speech reflect God's grace to the world? You may want to jot down your answer underneath each of the verses.

17. Paul wrote that our words should be full of grace (Colossians 4:4-5). Why?

Who are the outsiders that Paul is referring to in these verses?

18. How are Jesus' words described in Luke 4:22 and John 1:14?

19. Read Ephesians 2:6-10. What does Paul teach the Ephesians about grace in these verses?

20. Suppose someone does not deserve to be spoken to with gracious words. Read Romans 3:23-24. By what means are we saved?

Read Romans 11:6. How does this verse explain that grace is something that is not earned or deserved? (Also see Galatians 2:21.)

21. Just how bad were we when God chose to extend grace to us and save us? Look up the following verses to see.

Before I knew Christ I was...

Ephesians 2:1

Ephesians 2:3

Ephesians 2:12

Ephesians 2:13

Ephesians 5:8

Colossians 1:21

22. I am still amazed that God would choose to shower His grace
on such an undeserving creature like me, but that's what grace
is all about. Ponder Romans 5:8 from the Amplified Version of
the Bible.

"But God shows and clearly proves His [own] love for us by the
fact that while we were still sinners, Christ (the Messiah, the
Anointed One) died for us."

God did not wait for us to clean up our act or get our life in
order. No, He knew that without the power of the Holy Spirit
we were unable to do either. It was while we were still living in
sin that God called us to Himself. My heart soars with John
Newton in the words to his most treasured hymn…

> *Amazing grace! how sweet the sound*
> *That saved a wretch like me!*
> *I once was lost, but now I'm found;*
> *Was blind, but now I see.*

23. A friend of mine had her purse stolen. Along with her cash,
driver's license, and credit cards was her phone bill. Because the
phone bill was taken, she forgot all about it and failed to pay it.
Several weeks later she received a letter from the company that
stated: "Because you have been a faithful customer, in light of
your delinquency in paying your bill, we will extend to you a
grace period."

Then there were two dates.

Grace period begins...

Grace period ends.

Aren't you glad that with Jesus, there is no end to our grace period? Likewise, we should extend that same grace to others with our words. After looking at these verses about God's grace, how do you think His grace should affect our speech to those who don't "deserve" graciousness?

24. Give an example of ways your words can be supernaturally gracious to others.

25. Is there anything you need to change to make your words more gracious and kind?

26. If there is anything I love, it is a pedicure. I tend to pay very little attention to my feet, but occasionally I'll hand them over to a professional, and she rubs, massages, sloughs, and paints until my feet are fresh and feminine again.

In the Bible, God tells us a beauty secret to having beautiful feet. Read Romans 10:11-15 and fill in the blank.

"How beautiful are the feet of those who bring _____ _____."

How does Isaiah 52:7 explain "good news"?

What did the angels bring to the shepherds in Luke 2:10?

"But the angel said to them, 'Do not be afraid. I bring you _____ _____of great joy that will be for all the people.'"

Continue reading in Luke 2. What was the "good news"?

In biblical times, messengers ran from the battlefields to inform anxious family and friends about the progress of the war. There was no more beautiful sight than an approaching messenger proclaiming, "Your God reigns! The battle is going in your favor!" Likewise, we can have the feet of a beautiful messenger when we run from the battlefields of life proclaiming to fellow soldiers, family, and friends, "Your God reigns! The battle is the Lord's!"

27. What was Jesus' message called? Matthew 4:23; 9:35; 11:5

What did Jesus command us to do? Mark 16:15

How did the early church put this into practice? Acts 5:42

28. *Vine's Complete Expository Dictionary of Old and New Testament Words* tells us the following about the word "gospel."

> Originally denoted a reward for good tidings; later, the idea of reward dropped, and the word stood for "the good news" itself. The English word "gospel," i.e. "good message," is the equivalent of euangelion. In the New Testament it denotes the "good tidings" of the kingdom of God and of salvation through Christ, to be received by faith, on the basis of His expiatory death, His burial, resurrection, and ascension.*

Friend, your feet are never more beautiful than when you are using your words to bring the good news of Jesus Christ to a hurting world.

As we complete this lesson for today, I pray that you will "grow in the grace and knowledge of our Lord and Savior Jesus Christ. To him be the glory both now and forever! Amen" (2 Peter 3:18).

---

* W.E. Vine, Merrill F. Unger, and William White Jr., *Vines' Complete Expository Dictionary of Old and New Testament Words* (Nashville: Thomas Nelson Publishers, 1985), p. 275.

The Power of a Woman's Words to God

Power verse:
*"The prayer of a righteous person
is powerful and effective."*

JAMES 5:17 TNIV

EVERY DAY WE HAVE the opportunity to impact the people in our lives, for good or evil, with the words we speak. We can breathe life into those in need of a bit of resuscitation or suck the wind out of their sails. We affect others by the words that come out of our mouths.

However, the words we speak to God have a direct impact on *our own* lives. God invites us to join in conversation with Him. Isn't that astounding? The God of the universe longs for you and me to talk to Him. And when we talk to God, He talks to us.

In this lesson let's take a look at the power of our words to God and His power that flows back to us.

1. What is the purpose of prayer? I think David gives us one of many answers to that question in Psalm 25:2-5. Read and record your findings.

2. God is sovereign. He is in total control and has a preordained plan. Prayer is not to change God's mind, but to align our thinking with His. It is not a "wish list," but an attitude of submission to God, communication with God, and receptivity to God. What do the following verses teach about the sovereignty of God?

Psalm 33:11

Psalm 115:3

Ecclesiastes 3:14

Jeremiah 29:11

3. God is sovereign, and yet all through the Bible we see God seemingly change the course of His actions because of someone's prayer.

Read Exodus 32:7-14 and answer the following questions.

How had the Israelites angered God?

What was He going to do?

How did Moses avert God's anger?

4. How do we reconcile the truth of God's sovereignty with the obvious effect of intercessory prayer in the Bible? ("Intercessory prayer" is praying for another person or "interceding" for them.)

    That is a question that will not be answered in this Bible study. As a matter of fact, that question has been debated by biblical scholars for hundreds of years. This is all I know: God is sovereign, and yet He calls us to intercessory prayer. It seems to me that there are natural consequences or courses of action that God has set in motion. For example: If you disobey, you are punished. Eve ate the forbidden fruit, and she suffered the consequences. However, intercessory prayer can stop the natural course of action with supernatural intervention by God.

    Think about that last sentence and write down your thoughts.

5. God is looking for intercessors to pray! That could be you. Read Ezekiel 22:23-31 and answer the following questions.

    Why was God angry at the nation of Israel?

    What or who was He looking for in verse 30?

    God was looking for someone to "stand in the gap"—to pray

for Israel—but there was no one willing to pray. We can "stand in the gap" for the people in our lives. We can use our words to pray for God's mercy, intervention, salvation, healing, and restoration. He is looking for someone to stand in the gap!

6. God's Word is very visual. The Lord paints word pictures to help us understand spiritual principles. God could have said, "I couldn't find anyone to pray," but He said, "I couldn't find anyone to stand in the gap." Use the space below to draw a picture of the image that comes to mind when you read the words "stand in the gap" in regard to prayer.

7. Let's look at the power of our words to pray for others or intercede for them. Read and note what you learn about the power of intercessory prayer in these New Testament verses.

Matthew 18:18-19

James 5:16

8. Prayer is like a key that unlocks God's power. How is that idea described in Ephesians 3:20?

Prayerless lives are powerless lives.

Prayerful lives are powerful lives.

9. God knows what we need before we need it, and yet He tells us to pray. Read the following verses and write what you learn.

Psalm 139:4

Matthew 6:8

Matthew 7:7

1 Thessalonians 5:17

James 4:2

From these verses, what is your understanding of God's power released through prayer?

10. Yes, there is power in a woman's words to God, but let's not ever

forget where that power comes from. Read and record 2 Corinthians 4:7.

Some of us may feel like a "cracked pot" or clay jar. That's okay. That just means the light of Christ can shine through those cracks!

11. Prayer transcends the physical realm of what we can see with our eyes and travels to the spiritual realm, which is temporarily veiled. What does Ephesians 6:10-12 tell us about the spiritual battle that rages around us?

12. Elisha got a peek into that realm. What did he and his servant see when God temporarily removed the veil that separates the physical and the spiritual? 2 Kings 6:8-17

Elisha knew by faith that the angels were surrounding them. We have that same assurance (Hebrews 1:1). What do you learn from this verse?

13. Did you know that the devil has a scheme as mentioned in Ephesians 6:10-12? The word "scheme" means "a well-thought-out plan." He has carefully crafted ways to destroy mankind and keep them from experiencing the peace and joy God intended. But what is the promise of 1 John 4:4? Read and record that powerful promise.

14. Whenever you see the word "therefore" in Scripture, it links together a cause and an effect. Read Ephesians 6:10-12 again.

    What is the cause? (The problem)

    What is the effect? (The solution)

    What is Paul's summary of our action steps for prayer? Ephesians 6:18

15. It is easy to read about the powerful prayers of mighty men and women in the Bible and think they had some inside line to God. However, what do we learn about Elijah in James 5:17-18?

    "He was a man _____."

    How can you apply that verse to your own life?

16. Jesus knew the power of prayer. He talked to His heavenly Father often. Read the following and note what you learn about Jesus' times of prayer.

    Matthew 26:36-46

    Luke 5:16

Luke 6:12

Luke 9:18

Luke 9:29

Summarize what you learned about Jesus' dependence on prayer.

17. There are many aspects to prayer: thanking God for what He has done, praising God for who He is, confession of sin, intercession for others, requests for our own needs. The prayer that Jesus taught His disciples to pray included each of these elements (Matthew 6:9-15; Luke 11:2-4). Let's look at the power that is released from our words of praise and thanksgiving. Read Acts 16:16-40 and note the difficult situation of Paul and Silas. Rather than complain, what did they begin to do? Acts 16:25

What was the result of their praises to God? Acts 16:26-34.

Who was set free?

Did you notice the effect Paul and Silas' praises to God had on those around them? How could your words to God affect those around you?

18. What do the following verses teach about the power of praising God?

    Psalm 50:14-15

    Psalm 107:21-22

    Hebrews 13:15

19. God also invites us to talk to Him about our needs. Read the following and note what you learn.

    Matthew 21:22

    Mark 9:29

    Mark 11:24

James 5:15-16

20. Paul was a man of prayer and constantly prayed for his friends. Read the following passages of Scripture and note exactly what Paul prayed.

Ephesians 1:15-23

Ephesians 3:14-20

Philippians 1:3-6

Philippians 1:9-11

Colossians 1:3-12

21. We can use these same passages of Scripture as a powerful pattern of prayer. For example, choose a person for whom you would like to intercede and pray one of the above Scriptures over him or her.

Let's put into practice what we've learned in this lesson and pray. Pray Colossians 1:9-12 over someone you love and stand in the gap for him or her today.

Dear Lord, I pray for (_____) today and ask that You fill him with the knowledge of Your will through all spiritual wisdom and understanding. I pray this in order that (_____) may live a life worthy of the Lord and may please You in every way; bearing fruit in every good work, growing in the knowledge of God, being strengthened with all power according to Your glorious might so that (_____) may have great endurance and patience and joyfully giving thanks to God, who has qualified (_____) to share in the inheritance of the saints in the kingdom of light. In Jesus' name, amen.

Lesson 10

THE PROMISE OF POWER

Power verse:

"I pray also that the eyes of your heart may be enlightened in order that you may know the hope to which he has called you, the riches of his glorious inheritance in the saints, and his incomparably great power for us who believe."

EPHESIANS 1:18-19

JUST AS IT TAKES MANY MACHINES working in tandem to light up a city, there are many facets to the source of our power to change. First, let's look at the power of the Holy Spirit that has been given to every believer.

1. Read John 14 and note everything you learn about the Holy Spirit.

2. The Greek word most often used in the New Testament for the Holy Spirit comes from the verb *parakaleo*, which means "to come alongside."

   The New Testament word most often translated as "encouragement" is *parakalein*. The word comes from two Greek words:

para, meaning "alongside of," and *kaleo*, meaning "to call." Do these two Greek words shed any light on your understanding of the Holy Spirit and what He does? If so, explain.

3. Jesus warned the disciples not to begin their post-resurrection ministry without the power of the Holy Spirit. To refresh your memory, how did Peter stand up against the pressure during Jesus' arrest and trial? Matthew 26:69-74

4. Describe the scene in Acts 2.

Speaking in tongues is a very controversial subject. Please don't get bogged down on this point. However, I do want you to answer this question: What was the first evidence of the power of the Holy Spirit working in the believers?

I hope you said their words!

The Holy Spirit infuses us with power from on high, and He works in tandem with Jesus to strengthen us. While the power comes from God, He requires our cooperation.

5. After the infilling of the Holy Spirit, Peter was a changed and spiritually charged man. Compare the Peter in Acts 2:14-40 with the Peter we met in Matthew 26:69-74. How was he different?

What was the result of Peter's powerful sermon? Acts 2:41

6. Just before Jesus' arrest, He told the disciples the family secret to success. Summarize His teaching on "abiding" or "remaining" in the vine (John 15:1-17). Note how many times He repeated that one word.

7. The word "remain" or "abide" is from the Greek word *meno*. It means "to rest in, tarry on in, continue in, focus on, pursue in order to experience." I like to think of it as where my soul chooses to dwell. What word picture comes to mind when you think of abiding in Christ?

8. The word "abide" or "remain" is not a suggestion. It is a command. You don't have to command someone to do something that comes naturally. You do not have to command a child to eat ice cream. Why do you think Jesus was so adamant about abiding? Do you think it comes naturally for us?

9. Answer the following questions from John 15:1-17.

Who is the vine? What is the purpose of the vine?

Who is the vinedresser? What is the job of the vinedresser?

Who are the branches? What is the purpose of a branch?

What is the fruit?

10. If you are doing this study in a group, you might have heard several different answers for what the "fruit" represents. Read the following verses and note what you learn about fruit.

Matthew 12:33: Fruit represents _____.

Luke 3:8: Fruit represents _____.

John 4:34-38: Fruit (or harvest) represents _____.

John 15:16: Fruit represents _____.

Galatians 5:22-23: Fruit represents _____.

How are each of these examples of "fruit" a product of our words?

11. In John 15, Jesus told the disciples, "Every branch that bears fruit He prunes, that it may bear more fruit" (verse 2 NKJV). I'm not too crazy about the idea of being pruned, but I get very excited about the possibility of bearing more fruit for Christ. What happens if you do not prune roses or other flowering plants?

Have you ever grown plants that needed pruning? If so, what happens when you do not prune and what happens when you do prune?

No matter where we fall on the continuum of speaking wise words and foolish words, there is always room for improvement. I pray that God will prune away the unhealthy words from our lives so that we will produce a bountiful harvest of delicious, flavorful fruit.

12. Bruce Wilkerson, in his book *Secrets of the Vine,* notes this about pruning:

> Looking at the branch in Jesus' hand that night, the disciples knew exactly what He meant by pruning...They understood that to get more from a grapevine, you have to *go against the plant's natural tendency.* Left to itself, a grape plant will always favor new growth over more grapes. The result? From a distance, luxurious growth, and impressive achievement. Up close, an underwhelming harvest. That's why the vinedresser cuts away unnecessary shoots, no matter how vigorous, because a vineyard's only purpose is...grapes. In fact, pruning is a grower's single most important technique for ensuring a plentiful harvest.*

What is the natural tendency of a grapevine?

What is the natural tendency for our speech?

---

* Bruce Wilkerson, *Secrets of the Vine* (Sisters, OR: Multnomah Publishers, Inc., 2001), pp. 58-59.

How does God prune us?

What is His desire for our words?

13. If I were with you right now, I'd pull up a chair and not sit in it, but stand on it to make this point unforgettable. Read John 15:5 once again and fill in the blank.

"I am the vine; you are the branches. If a man remains in me and I in him, he will bear much fruit; apart from me you can do _____."

When we do not abide in Jesus, we can be very busy, but we will not bear fruit that remains. He gives us the power through the Holy Spirit to transform our speech into a bountiful harvest of wise words. Without Him, we simply will not succeed.

14. Martha was a woman who was very busy but not very fruitful. Jesus reminded her what was important and invited her to tap into the power source for change. Read Luke 10:38-42 and answer the following questions.

What was Martha's dilemma?

Where was Mary?

How did Martha's words reveal what was in her heart?

What was Jesus' response to Martha?

15. Mary was one of the first women theologians who sat at Jesus' feet. That was a cultural enigma. Women did not sit with the men to hear great teachers, and yet Jesus welcomed her and said, "It will not be taken away from her." Now let's fast forward several months. Read John 11:1-27. (I just have to point out one little phrase. For centuries, scholars have used Martha as a bad example, but what does John tell us about how Jesus felt about Martha in John 11:5? So there you have it! He loved her.)

Describe the scene.

What did Martha say when she met Jesus? John 11:21-22,27

What did Martha's words reveal about her faith?

What transformation do you see in Martha's faith and speech from the first scene and the second?

How do you think this transformation took place?

I believe that Martha heeded Jesus' words and began to sit at His feet with her sister. Somewhere between the kitchen and the funeral, she realized who Jesus was and what He could do. By spending time with Jesus, even her speech changed from fretful to faithful.

16. How has the realization of who Jesus is changed your life?

How has the realization of who Jesus is affected your speech? Has He transformed you from fretful to faithful?

17. I am going to take you now to a difficult passage in the Bible. Read Luke 11:24-26.

It appears that this man had "cleaned up his act." Perhaps Jesus is referring to the Jewish exorcists who cast out demons. But once the house was empty, what did he fail to do?

It is not enough to clean out the house. We have to make sure that someone takes up residence and there is a "No Vacancy" sign posted on the door of our hearts. I believe Jesus is explaining what happens when someone tries to live morally without the regeneration of the spirit that comes with a relationship with Jesus Christ—without the Holy Spirit taking up residence.

18. Who indwells the believer? John 14:20; Acts 2:4; Ephesians 5:18

19. What is the promise of power found in Philippians 4:13?

20. Sometimes we fall into the trap of thinking that the heroes of the faith in the Bible were different from you and me. However, they were men and women who struggled with the same inner conflicts that we wrestle with today. Read Romans 7:7-24 and summarize Paul's dilemma.

    Paul was a miserable man when he tried to live a godly life apart from the power of the Holy Spirit. He could not do it in his own strength. He was so excited to tell us the answer to his miserable existence he couldn't even wait until chapter 8. What was the solution to Paul's struggle and to our struggle recorded in verse 7:25?

21. In reality, where does our power to change come from? Read and note the following.

    2 Corinthians 4:7

    Philippians 2:13

    2 Peter 1:3-4

22. Did you realize that when you became a Christian, God transformed you into a new creation? Read the following verses and note who you really are as a child of God and the power that lives within you.

John 14:20

Romans 6:18

2 Corinthians 5:17

Philippians 4:13

23. With your new identity, you have received great power! Read the following verses and note the magnitude of the power of the Holy Spirit that lives within you.

Romans 15:13

2 Corinthians 4:7

2 Corinthians 10:4

24. Today's power verse is power packed. Read Ephesians 1:18-21 again. Complete verse 19:

"That power is like _____

_____

_____."

How does Paul describe that power that lives within you?

Go back up to verse 19. Who has this power been given to?

Please note the "those who believe" is a present-tense verb. It is not those who "believed" as in Ephesians 1:13. The past tense "believed" implies a point in time at which we believed on Jesus Christ as Lord and Savior and are saved. However, the present tense "believe" implies the continual process of believing God day after day.

25. What does present-tense believing mean to you?

From this verse, why is present-tense believing crucial to the power we possess?

26. What does Matthew 17:20 tell us about the mountain-moving power our words possess?

If you are a Christian, you possess the power of the Holy Spirit to change the way you speak. It involves believing, and it also involves practicing, but we'll get to that in the next lesson. However, we can never act beyond what we believe, so we must believe we have the power of the Holy Spirit working in us before we can change.

27. Do you believe? If you believe you have the power of the Holy Spirit working in your life to tame the tongue, then write out your statement of faith.

I believe _____

_____

_____ .

28. Jesus gives us the ultimate example of how to use our words. What did He tell us in Matthew 11:29?

"_____ upon you."

"_____ from me."

When a farmer was training a young ox in biblical times, he would yoke the young ox to an older, trained ox. The older ox did all the work, but the younger ox followed alongside his "mentor" and learned how to plow. That is the same picture Jesus paints as we are yoked to our teacher. He does the work as we walk in tandem with Him. What would happen if the young ox ran ahead of the older ox and pulled on the yoke?

What would happen if the younger ox lagged behind and the older ox had to pull him along?

I don't want my neck to chafe because of running ahead or lagging behind! When we walk in tandem with Jesus, yoked to the Master teacher, we can learn how to use our words as God intended. The Holy Spirit gives the power. Jesus gives the example.

29. What does Jesus promise us in Luke 6:40?

What is our responsibility in this process?

30. How did Jesus know what to say at any given time? John 14:24; 17:8

What a wonderful example of one of my new resolves: "Don't speak unless you are spoken through."

31. To summarize what we have learned so far about the power to change the words we speak, circle the appropriate answer.

Apart from Christ I can/cannot consistently and permanently change the way I speak.

Through Christ I can/cannot consistently and permanently change the way I speak.

THE PRODUCT OF PRACTICE

Power verse:

*"Let your conversation be always full of grace,
seasoned with salt, so that you may
know how to answer everyone."*

COLOSSIANS 4:6

I AM SO GLAD that I don't have to try and change the way I speak on my own. I've tried it. I failed. However, as we learned in the last lesson, we are not alone in this battle for the control of our tongues. We have the power of the Holy Spirit working in us. James said that it was impossible to tame the tongue. Yes, it is impossible in our own strength. But as the angel reminded Mary, the mother of Jesus, "Nothing is impossible with God" (Luke 1:37). In this lesson, we will get specific about changing various aspects of the words we speak. Let's get started!

1. Read 2 Corinthians 5:17. What does Paul say happens to us when we become a Christian?

2. I hope you wrote down that we become new creations. But while our spirits do become brand-new, no one pushes the "delete" button on our old habit patterns. What must we do to make

our actions line up with our new identity? Read Romans 12:2 and fill in the blanks.

"Do not conform any longer to the pattern of this world, but be _____ by the _____ of your mind. Then you will be able to test and approve what God's will is—his good, pleasing and perfect will."

How do you renew your mind? There are many ways. List five.

1.

2.

3.

4.

5.

3. First we reprogram our minds and then we practice what we learn. We must work in tandem with the Holy Spirit. Read Ephesians 4:22-32 and list what we are to "put off" and "put on."

We are to put off:

We are to put on:

4. Now read Colossians 3:5-17 and follow the same process.

   We are to put off:

   We are to put on:

5. To "put off" means to "strip off as in the case of filthy clothes." How does this relate to the words we speak?

6. Read Romans 6:11-13 and answer the following questions.

   Verse 13 tells us to offer the members of our bodies to God. How does this relate to our power verse for today?

   These verses are so important, let's ponder them for a moment. Go back and read Romans 6:8-10 for a better understanding.

   Paul asks us to ponder this question: If the old self is dead, then why do we continue to struggle with sin and how can we learn to let the new self become dominant? He gives two directives:

   1. Count yourselves dead to sin. This is saying with unreserved confidence that the old self is dead. It is a statement of faith in which we embrace what our

minds know to be true. "I am a new creation in Christ"
(2 Corinthians 5:17).

2. Count yourselves alive to God. Again, by faith I am
risen with Christ, have the mind of Christ, and have
the spirit of Christ living in me.

That is what I believe and confess. Now, there is an action
required as well...the offering of the members of our bodies to
God or to sin. That's where daily choices affect the moments
of our days.

7. Read Psalm 119:11. What did David do in order to deter sin in
his life?

The word "hidden" means "to treasure, hide, protect, hoard,
reserve." The same word is used of Moses' mother, who hid him
from Pharaoh for three months.*

How can you hide God's Word in your heart?

8. Like any new habit, change takes practice and discipline. The
Greek word for "discipline" is *gumnazo*. It means "to exercise or
train." The English word "gymnastics" comes from the Greek
word *gumnazo*. How is changing the way you speak like working
out at the gym?

---

* Rhonda Rizzo Webb, *Words Begin in Our Hearts* (Chicago, IL: Moody Publishers, 2003), p. 16.

Charles Spurgeon said, "Jesus is more ready to pardon than you are to sin, more willing to supply your wants than you are to confess them. Never tolerate low thoughts of Him. You may study, look, and meditate, but Jesus is a greater Savior than you think Him to be—when your thoughts are their highest."

9. Note the following verse.

"Do not let any unwholesome talk come out of your mouths, but only what is helpful for building others up according to their needs, that it may benefit those who listen" (Ephesians 4:29).

List four requirements for wholesome words listed in this verse.

1.

2.

3.

4.

What is unwholesome talk? You may want to look up the word "unwholesome" in a dictionary.

If you have access to a King James Version of the Bible, what word is used for "unwholesome"?

Look up that word in a dictionary.

Give an example of how passing your words by those four requirements might stop them from passing your lips.

10. Let's look at some specific ways to change.

Read Philippians 2:14-16 and fill in the blanks.

"Do everything without _____ or _____
you may become blameless and pure, children of God without
_____ in a crooked and depraved generation, in which
you _____ like _____ in the universe as you
hold out the word of life—in order that I may boast on the day
of Christ that I did not run or labor for nothing."

Look up and define the following:

Complaining:

Arguing:

11. When my son was a preschooler, he was a big whiner. Like a kid learning to play a violin, he whined about first one thing and then another. I can't stand whining. I'd often say, "Steven, stop whining. I'd rather hear you cry than whine." You'll be pleased to know that Steven is now a happy, successful young adult. These days, I whine more than he does.

How does God feel about our whining and grumbling? Numbers 14:27-30

When we complain, who are we ultimately complaining about? Exodus 16:6-7

12. When you don't feel like thanking God, that's when it becomes a "sacrifice of praise." What do the following verses say about a sacrifice of thanksgiving?

Psalm 107:21-22

Psalm 116:17

Hebrews 13:15-16

13. Read and note what you learn about thanksgiving in the following verses.

Ephesians 4:29-31

Ephesians 5:4

Philippians 2:14-15

Philippians 4:6

14. Corrie ten Boom was in a Nazi concentration camp during World War II. Her cabin was filled with fleas, and yet she taught her fellow inmates to praise God for the fleas. They had a difficult time believing that anything good could come from the constant torture of this parasite. Then one day they realized that the guards would not come into their cabin because of the fleas and Corrie was able to teach the gospel freely. What does this example show us about the power of praise?

15. Do you enjoy being around people who complain, grumble, or whine? Do you think people enjoy being around you when you complain, grumble, or whine? Read the following verses and come up with an anecdote for complaining.

Ephesians 5:20

Philippians 4:6

1 Thessalonians 5:18

16. The world is accustomed to complaining and grumbling. When a person does not complain or grumble, he or she actually stands out...they shine like stars in the universe.

What does Daniel 12:3 tell you about becoming a star?

What is Jesus called in Revelation 22:16?

Isn't it an amazing thought that by our words we can reflect the glory of God and shine like the Morning Star in a dark world? This is just one example of how changing the way we speak has a powerful influence on the people around us.

17. Let's look at some words that can eclipse the glow of a star.

NAGGING
Using a dictionary, define "nagging."

Look up the following verses and note what you learn about nagging.

Judges 16:16

Proverbs 21:19

MEDDLING
Using a dictionary, define "meddling."

Look up the following verses and note what you learn about meddling.

Proverbs 26:17

1 Timothy 5:13

BRAGGING

Using a dictionary, define "bragging."

Look up the following verses and note what you learn about bragging.

Proverbs 14:23

Proverbs 27:2

QUARRELLING

Using a dictionary, define "quarrelling."

Look up the following verses and note what you learn about quarrelling.

Proverbs 17:14

Proverbs 20:3

Proverbs 26:21

Proverbs 27:15

SWEARING or CURSING

Using a dictionary, define "swearing" and "cursing."

Look up the following verses and note what you learn about both.

Deuteronomy 5:11

Proverbs 4:24

Colossians 3:8

18. In order to avoid negative speech that is not pleasing to God or mankind, we must resolve to change and then pray that God will continually give us the power to do so. What did David say about his words in Psalm 17:3?

19. Daniel was a man who purposed in his heart not to follow the pagan ways of Babylon. I love comparing various translations

of the Bible to get insight into the original Hebrew language of the Old Testament. Compare these four translations of Daniel 1:8.

- "But Daniel *resolved* not to defile himself with the royal food and wine" (NIV).

- "But Daniel *made up his mind* that he would not defile himself with the king's choice food or with the wine which he drank" (NASB).

- "But Daniel *determined in his heart* that he would not defile himself by [eating his portion of] the king's rich and dainty food or with the wine which he drank" (AMP).

- "But Daniel *purposed in his heart* that he would not defile himself with the portion of the king's meat, nor with the wine which he drank" (KJV).

By comparing these four versions of the Bible, what synonyms or similar words can you use to describe what it means to "purpose" in your mind or heart?

20. Use this space to write your resolve about the words you speak.

I resolve, make up my mind, determine in my heart to

_____

_____.

Let's pray together for a moment.

Dear Father, many times my words are filled with grumbling and complaining. Sometimes I don't sound any different from the world around me...never satisfied, but always wanting more. Today, please convict me before the grumbling passes my lips. Help me "put my hand over my mouth," as Job so aptly put it. May the words of my mouth and the meditation of my heart be pleasing in Your sight and a light to those around me. Today, help me be a shining star. In Jesus' name, amen.

Lesson 12

THE POTENCY OF SILENCE

Power verse:

*"Set a guard over my mouth, O LORD;
keep watch over the door of my lips."*

PSALM 141:3

"I CAN'T BELIEVE I JUST SAID THAT!" How many times has this been your lament? It has been my cry on more occasions than I can even count. Sometimes it's very difficult to hold the tongue and remain silent. However, on many occasions, the most powerful words are the ones we don't say at all. Today, let's look at what the Bible reveals about the power of holding our tongues.

1. Read James 1:19 and note the three instructions.

Be quick _____

Be slow _____

Be slow _____

Isn't it interesting that the only "quick" action includes no words spoken?

2. Read and record Proverbs 4:23.

    When you think of a wellspring, what comes to mind? Draw
    a picture below.

    With that verse still in your mind, read James 3:10-12. Pretend
    that James is sitting right there with you and asking you those
    two rhetorical questions. Answer him.

    How do we keep the heart pure so that the words that flow out
    are pure?

3. What do the following verses say about guarding our words?
    Because we are doing a study on the power of a woman's words,
    let's change each "he" to "she." I don't think God will mind.

    Proverbs 9:13

    Proverbs 10:8

    Proverbs 10:19

Proverbs 11:12

Proverbs 11:22

Proverbs 13:3

Proverbs 14:3

Proverbs 17:27-28

Proverbs 18:2

Proverbs 21:23

Proverbs 29:20

Did you see yourself in any of those verses? If so, place a check mark by the verse.

4. Read and record Psalm 141:3.

David prayed that God would guard his heart, and he also prayed that God would set a guard over his mouth. What does it mean to guard our mouths?

What does a prison guard do?

How can we consider the role of a prison guard in relation to our words?

5. Tucked between the books of Nehemiah and Job rests a short book about the fate of a little orphaned Jewish girl who knew when to hold her tongue and when to speak. Let's take a look at how her wisdom to know the difference saved an entire nation. Read Esther 1 and write down everything you learn about King Xerxes. (Some Bible translations refer to him by his Hebrew name, Ahasuerus.)

On a scale of 1 to 10, how would you rate his power?

What was Queen Vashti's response to the king's request?

What was the result of her response?

6. We don't know why Vashti refused the king's request. Some

suppose that she did not want to parade in front of a room of drunken gawking men. Others proposed that the king wanted her to appear in her crown...only. In any case, her answer was no. How did the king's wise men and nobles view the power of the queen's words to affect the other women in the kingdom? (verses 16-18).

If you have children in your home, there are little eyes in your castle watching to see how you respond to the king (your husband). What are your children learning about honor and respect from the way you speak to your husband? Have you seen your words reflected in the attitudes of your children?

These wise men understood the power of a woman's words! What did they advise the king to do in response to the queen's actions?

7. Now let's move on to chapter 2. List everything you learn about Hadassah. Who was she? How was she described?

What do you learn about her ability to keep silent?

8. We aren't going to stop and study chapter 3, but it is necessary to keep the story in context. Read and summarize the events

that led to the decree to annihilate all the Jews on the thirteenth day of the twelfth month.

Who would be among those killed? (3:5-7)

9. In chapter 4, the plot thickens. What did Mordecai ask Esther to do? (4:7-8)

What was her dilemma? (4:10-11)

Read verses 12-14 and fill in the following blanks.

"For if you remain silent at this time, relief and deliverance for the Jews will arise from another place, but you and your father's family will perish. And who knows but that you

_____

_____."

What was Esther's response to Mordecai? (4:15-17)

10. Mordecai was teaching Esther a principle also found in Ecclesiastes 3:7. What does this verse tell us about timing?

11. Before Esther went before the king, what did she ask of Mordecai and her servants?

12. Read 5:1-8 and note Esther's approach to the king. Rather than beg for her people immediately, what did she do?

    How do you think she knew the timing wasn't right to reveal Haman's plot? (4:16)

13. To keep the story in context, read 5:9-6:14 and note any details that you find interesting.

14. Chapter 7 describes Esther's second dinner party with the king. This time, she reveals her true request. What evidences of her humble spirit do you see in her request?

    What do you think was the difference between how Esther made her request to the king and how Queen Vashti denied his request?

15. Skip down to 8:3-6 and again note her humble approach.

16. What was the outcome of Esther's bravery? (8:7-17)

Even today, the Jews celebrate Queen Esther's bravery at the Feast of Purim. The NIV commentary notes: "Against a background of centuries of persecution, it is understandable why Purim has become such a favorite of the Jews. It recalls a time when they were able to turn the tables on those who wanted to destroy them. Purim is celebrated today amid a carnival-like atmosphere, with masquerade parties, noisemaking, and revelry."*

17. The most powerful example of silence is found in the life and death of Jesus. Read 1 Peter 2:23 and note how Jesus faced His accusers.

    Is it difficult for you not to retaliate or defend yourself when spoken against?

18. One of the main reasons we try to defend ourselves is because we cling to the idea that we have "rights." Our culture is highly focused on personal rights—women's rights, gay rights, civil rights, animal rights, etc. But, unfortunately, the cornerstone for much of our beliefs in personal rights is pride. The Bible, on the other hand, teaches us to put aside our rights to become humble servants willing to sacrifice our personal rights for the betterment of others—not a very popular concept in our "me first" society. Read Philippians 2:5-8 and note how Jesus gave up His personal rights so that you and I could have eternal life.

    Jesus didn't have to give up His rights and remain silent during His persecution and crucifixion. He chose to remain silent. I cannot even imagine the amount of control that must have been

---

* Kenneth L. Barker and John R. Kohlenberger III, *Zondervan NIV Commentary Volume 1: Old Testament* (Grand Rapids, MI: Zondervan Publishing House, 1994), p. 726.

necessary for Him to not come down from that cross and claim His rightful place as King. However, He did not defend Himself but died for you instead. He loves you that much.

19. What does the realization of Jesus' humility mean to you?

How should that understanding of Jesus' humility affect the way we retaliate with our words?

20. God hates pride. It is the very thing that caused Satan to fall from heaven with a third of all the angels. Read the following and contrast "pride" and "humility." Use the chart on page 142 to record your findings.

Psalm 18:27

Psalm 25:9

Proverbs 3:34

Proverbs 11:2

Proverbs 16:18

Proverbs 22:4

Proverbs 29:23

Result of Pride	Result of Humility

21. Humility is not a sign of weakness. It is a sign of self-control—one of the mightiest forms of strength and power we can exhibit. Have you ever known a strong person who was also very humble? How would you describe their speech?

22. In closing, read and record Proverbs 18:12.

This has been a tough lesson. If you're like me, your toes are hurting a bit from being stepped on by the Holy Spirit. Let's pray together.

Dear Lord, You know that I am too quick to speak. Help me to be quick to hear and slow to speak. I pray You will help me to know when to speak and when to remain quiet. I do not need to voice every thought that comes into my head. Help me to weigh my answers carefully and use my words wisely, and, if need be, sparingly. I pray I will be like Esther, who waited for the right time to say the right words. Thank You, Father, that You have given me the power of the Holy Spirit to do all that You have called me to do...including controlling my tongue. In Jesus' name, amen.

*T*HE *P*ASSPORT TO *R*EFRESHING THE *S*OUL

Power verse:

*"Give, and it will be given to you. A good measure,
pressed down, shaken together and running over,
will be poured into your lap. For with the measure
you use, it will be measured to you."*

LUKE 6:38

IF YOU HAVE EVER FELT EMPTY, as though you had nothing to give, you are not alone. Perhaps you've wondered, *How can I encourage other people when I am the one who needs encouraging?* All through the Bible we see men and women who felt emotionally and spiritually empty, and yet God sent someone with encouraging words to fill them up.

1. Read John 4:4-42 and answer the following questions.

Why did Jesus go to Samaria?

Jews went to great lengths to avoid Samaria, a land of half-breeds. Rather than take the fastest route from along the coast, they often crossed the Jordan River to avoid the area altogether. So

Jesus didn't have to go to Samaria because of geography. Why do you think He *had* to go there? Read John 8:28 and John 12:50 for a clue.

2. What was His request of the Samaritan woman? (We're back to John 4 now.)

    Jesus is all-powerful. Did He actually *need* the woman to get Him a drink?

    Why do you think He asked her?

3. I imagine there was a hint of sarcasm in the woman's reply. However, Jesus was unruffled as her defensive feathers rose. She was ready to spar, but Jesus chose not to get in the ring. Did He let her attitude deter Him from His mission?

4. In what ways was the Samaritan woman being argumentative?

5. In what ways did Jesus ignore her arguments and stick to the matter at hand...her heart?

6. Before her transforming encounter with Jesus, how would you describe the Samaritan woman's words?

7. After her encounter with Jesus, how would you describe the Samaritan woman's words?

It's not in the Bible, but when this woman ran back to town, leaving her water pot by the well, I imagine Jesus threw back His head and laughed. This hardened woman became like an absentminded little child who left her lunchbox on the playground as she ran to tell her classmates what she had just seen.

8. What evidence do you see that her words had great power in her community after her encounter with Jesus?

9. Before her encounter with Jesus, this woman was empty, but after her encounter, she was overflowing with the good news! How does that relate to your encounter with Jesus?

If you are feeling a bit dry today, Jesus would love to meet with you and fill you to overflowing. Read John 7:37.

How is the Holy Spirit described?

Paint a word picture of the Holy Spirit running through your soul. (Example: The Holy Spirit flows through me like a mountain stream.)

10. Jesus refreshed the woman at the well by giving her living water. He also gives us an example of how to refresh others during His last supper with His disciples. Read John 13:1-17.

Jesus put a towel around his waist, filled a basin with water, and knelt to wash His disciples' feet. It was customary for the host of a party to arrange for someone to wash the dusty feet of his sandal-clad guests. However, at their last supper together in the upper room, no one had taken the role of servant to wash their feet...until Jesus rose to do so. I imagine the disciples were in stunned silence as their Lord and King held their dusty feet in His royal hands and tenderly washed away their filth. I suspect this was one time when they were all in stunned silence. (Except our friend Peter, of course.)

After Jesus finished washing their feet, what did He tell them? John 13:14-17

Travelers did not wear closed shoes as we do today, but open sandals. I imagine having your feet washed was very refreshing. How could using our words to refresh others be like biblical feet washing?

What are some ways that you can put on the towel of servanthood and metaphorically wash someone's feet with encouraging words of refreshment?

11. In 2 Kings, we meet a woman who was running on empty. Not only was she spiritually empty, but her cupboard was also bare. Read 2 Kings 4:1-7 and answer the following questions.

    What was the widow's dilemma?

    What did Elisha ask her to do? Fill in the blanks.

    "Go around and ask all your neighbors for empty jars. Don't ask _____ _____ ____ _____."

    Hold that thought. We'll come back to it in a moment.

    Verse 4 has instructions that deserve pondering. Where did Elisha tell the woman to go?

    Sometimes God wants you all to Himself. He wants you to "go inside and shut the door behind you." Yes, He uses other people to lift our spirits and fill our empty emotional tanks, but sometimes, He wants to do it all by Himself! This miracle was not intended as a public demonstration, but as a personal display of God's love and mercy to this lone widow.

    Have you ever felt God calling you to "go inside and shut the door behind you"? If you are feeling empty today and there are no encouraging words left to overflow to anyone, go to the only One who can truly fill you to overflowing...the only One who can give you rivers of living water.

12. How many of the jars were filled?

    We don't know how many empty jars the boys brought to their

mom, but we do know how many were filled. What does this teach us about what we bring to God? How much of our emptiness will He fill?

God used what she had and filled up what she offered.

13. What does Paul tell us to do in Ephesians 5:18?

Why do you think Paul contrasted being filled with the Spirit and being filled with wine? What is the result of both of these "intoxications"?

The verb tense for "be filled" is present tense, which better translates, "be filled and continue being filled." When you are feeling empty and that you need refreshment in order to refresh others, pray that God will fill you anew with the power of His Holy Spirit.

14. In *The Power of a Woman's Words,* we learned how David refreshed himself in God. Read and record 1 Samuel 30:6.

David also refreshed his soul by speaking truth to himself. Read the following verses and note how David spoke truth into his soul to refresh himself.

Psalm 32:5

Psalm 42:11

Psalm 43:5 (Sometimes we have to say the same thing to our soul time and time again!)

Psalm 57:8-11

Psalm 62:5-6

Psalm 103:1-2,22

Psalm 116:7

Do you see a common theme or themes in what David spoke to his soul?

The soul consists of the mind, will, and emotions.

- David spoke Scripture to his mind to change the way he thought.

- David spoke Scripture to his will to change the way he acted.

- David spoke Scripture to his emotions to change the way he felt.

15. Jesus knew His disciples needed times of refreshment after an arduous day of ministry. Read the following verses and note how Jesus encouraged His disciples to rest and refuel.

Mark 6:30-32

16. Even Jesus needed to have times of refreshment with His heavenly Father. Read the following and note what you learn about Jesus' times alone.

Matthew 14:6-13

Mark 1:35

Luke 4:42

What do you think Jesus was doing during those times of solitude?

Read Luke 4:42-44. After Jesus' time of refreshment, what was He ready to do?

17. Yes, we use our words to encourage and refresh others. Ministry that does not come out of an overflow will lead to an undertow. However, an amazing thing happens when we give to others... God fills us up. Have you ever had a situation where you helped someone else, and yet you are the one who was blessed? If so, explain.

18. Read today's power verse again and note what you learn about giving to others. What is the result?

This verse is most often quoted in the context of giving financially. However, if you notice the verses before and after, Jesus was teaching about relationships. Luke 6:38 may very well apply to giving financially, but it most definitely applies to giving of ourselves in relationship to others. How does Luke 6:38 apply to the words we speak?

19. In closing, read and record Proverbs 11:25.

THE *P*ROFOUND *P*OSSIBILITIES*

Power verse:

"May the words of my mouth and the meditation of my heart be pleasing in your sight, O Lord, my Rock and my Redeemer."

Psalm 19:14

PLEASE KNOW THAT I LOVE YOU DEARLY, but I am getting ready to ask you some very tough questions. We will not grow in grace by reading one more book, attending one more class, or listening to one more speaker. We will grow in grace when we apply the truths that we already know.

1. Read the following and fill in the blanks.

    "Only let us _____ up to what we have already attained" (Philippians 3:16).

    "Anyone who listens to the word but _____ what it says is like a man who looks at his face in a mirror and, after looking at himself, goes away and immediately forgets what he looks like. But the man who looks intently into the perfect law that gives freedom, and _____ this, not forgetting

---

* This lesson is somewhat shorter than the other lessons. I hope you will take this time to share with your group or journal your thoughts about what you have learned about the power of a woman's words through this study.

what he has heard, but _____—he will be blessed in what he does" (James 1:23-25).

"We know that we have come to know him if we _____ his commands. The man who says, 'I know him,' but does not do what he commands is a liar, and the truth is not in him. But if anyone _____ his word, God's love is truly made complete in him. This is how we know we are in him: Whoever claims to live in him must _____ as Jesus did" (1 John 2:3-6).

2. As we learned in lesson 11, the Greek work for "discipline" is *gumnazo* which means "to exercise or train." It closely resembles the English word "gymnasium."

   What do the following verses teach us about discipline? Think about discipline in terms of training rather than punishment.

   Proverbs 10:17

   Proverbs 13:18

3. Closely tied to discipline is practice. What do the following verses teach us about practicing what we have learned?

   Luke 6:47-49

   Luke 8:21

   Philippians 4:9

The more we practice using our words to be a blessing to those around us, the easier it will become. The more we practice abstaining from using our words in a negative way, the easier taming and holding the tongue will become.

Learning how to use the power of your words for good is a process. It doesn't happen overnight. My dictionary defines "process" as "a natural phenomenon marked by gradual changes that lead toward a particular result; a series of actions or operations conducing to an end."

4. God has entrusted us with a powerful gift—the gift of words. It is a treasure He wants us to use wisely. Read Matthew 25:14-30 and answer the following questions.

    How did the master determine how much to give each servant?

    Was he more pleased with the one who had ten or the one who had four?

    I hope you said he was equally pleased. It doesn't matter the amount of the return. What mattered is that both were faithful with what they had been given.

    What did the servant who had one talent do?

    Did he have the ability to invest? (See Matthew 25:15.)

Why didn't he invest the talent? (See Matthew 25:25.) Give your answer in one word.

Oh, friend, we should never withhold a word of encouragement because we are afraid or embarrassed. God will put people in our paths who need a word of blessing. They are longing for someone to invest in them. He has given you treasures (Colossians 2:3), filled you to all the fullness of Christ (Colossians 2:10), and blessed you with every spiritual blessing in the heavenly realm (Ephesians 1:3). Now we are to invest in others with the lavish blessings God has given us. What are some ways you can use your words to invest in others?

I hope we may one day hear the words, "Well done, good and faithful servant" (Matthew 25:23).

5. After God promised Moses that He would speak through him, what did He tell him to do? Exodus 4:12

   After God cleansed Isaiah's lips, what did Isaiah agree to do? Isaiah 6:8

   What did God promise Isaiah? Isaiah 59:21

6. What were Jesus' final words to the disciples? Acts 1:7-8

And, friend, that is my final word to you. Go. Go in the power of the Holy Spirit, and may the power of your words spread the good news of Jesus Christ to those who cross your path.

In 1646 a group of theologians in England got together to answer some of the most important questions of the Christian faith. The first question was: What is the chief end of man? The answer: To glorify God and enjoy Him forever. Let's glorify God with our words and enjoy Him forever!

If you have any special thoughts on the power of your words that you would like to record in this workbook or a prayer you would like to write and keep, then please use the following lines.

_____

_____

_____

_____

_____

_____

_____

_____

_____

_____

_____

About the Author

Sharon Jaynes is an international inspirational speaker and Bible teacher for women's conferences and events. She is also the author of several books, including *Becoming the Woman of His Dreams, Becoming a Woman Who Listens to God, Experience the Ultimate Makeover,* and *Your Scars Are Beautiful to God.* Her books have been translated into several foreign languages and impacted women all around the globe. Sharon and her husband, Steve, live in North Carolina and have one grown son, Steven.

Sharon is always honored to hear from her readers. Please write to her directly at: *Sharon@sharonjaynes.com* or at her mailing address:

Sharon Jaynes
P.O. Box 725
Matthews, North Carolina 28106

To learn more about Sharon's books and speaking ministry or to inquire about having Sharon speak at your next event, visit

www.sharonjaynes.com.

HARVEST HOUSE
PUBLISHERS